CRACKING

Med School Admissions

2nd Edition

Rachel Rizal, MD; Rishi Mediratta, MD;
James Xie, MD; Devin Nambiar

1

TABLE OF CONTENTS

Have questions or need advice?

Contact the *Cracking Med School Admissions* team!

info@crackingmedadmissions.com

ABOUT THE AUTHORS

Rachel Rizal grew up in Cerritos, California. She has always had a strong interest in healthcare and education. Since high school, Rachel has advised hundreds of individuals for college, graduate school, scholarship, and fellowship applications. In high school, she was inducted to *USA Today's* All-USA High School Academic First Team for her international education work and recognized as a Coca-Cola Scholar. She attended Princeton for undergrad, and graduated cum laude from the Woodrow Wilson School of Public and International Affairs. There, she founded an organization called Health Matters, which creatively taught health education and brought medical resources to low-income families. After college, she pursued a Fulbright Fellowship where she led research and public health projects related to vaccinations and infectious diseases. Rachel received her M.D. at Stanford. She started a health education program in Stanford's Emergency Department and continued her vaccination work by leading Flu Crew, an organization that distributes free flu immunizations. She also worked for Stanford Health Care, learning hospital administration and business operations under the tutelage of the CEO, COO, and Vice Presidents of the hospital. Currently, Rachel is a resident in Emergency Medicine at Harvard. She advises non-profits and companies that focus on improving access to care, care coordination, and health education. She has a passion for interdisciplinary work, and wants to pursue a career that integrates medicine, public health, public policy, and business.
Contact Rachel at info@crackingmedadmissions.com

About The Authors

Rishi P. Mediratta grew up in Portage, Michigan and has lived and worked in London, Geneva, and Ethiopia, focusing on a wide-range of public health issues. He graduated Phi Beta Kappa with a degree in public health from the Johns Hopkins University where he developed medical and public health programs focused on preventing child mortality. Rishi's passion is designing and implementing sustainable programs. While living in Ethiopia, he founded the Ethiopian Orphan Health Foundation, a non-profit that provides community-based health care and education to vulnerable children. As a Marshall Scholar, he further examined the implications of delivering primary care services to children from an anthropological and a public health lens. Rishi integrates his field experience and interdisciplinary background to create child health programs and policies; he has worked with policymakers at the World Bank, the World Health Organization, and the Michigan Department of Community Health. Rishi received his M.D. at Stanford Medical School where he continued to spearhead initiatives to improve population health, primary care opportunities, and global health. He completed his Pediatrics residency at Stanford and is a faculty member at Stanford University School of Medicine. He continues to do research and global health work. He advises medical school and fellowship applicants and is a member of Stanford's Rhodes-Marshall Selection Committee.

Contact Rishi at info@crackingmedadmissions.com

ABOUT THE AUTHORS

James Xie has an international background: born in Bern, Switzerland, and raised for 10 years in the United Kingdom, before moving to the San Francisco Bay Area. He graduated with honors with a degree in Computer Science from Stanford. As the lead developer of Stanford Online, he improved online education resources and helped launch Stanford Engineering Everywhere, Stanford's free courseware initiative. He merged his interest in medicine with technology after working on the Healthy People 2020 national health policy document while in Washington D.C., and continued to work on health IT projects when back on campus. James received his M.D. from Stanford Medical School. There, he co-chaired the implementation of an electronic medical record for the student run Cardinal Free Clinics – one of the first student run free clinic systems to have a fully functioning EMR system in the nation. Teaching, educating, and mentoring are priorities in James' life – having been a teaching assistant in the clinical skills course for first year medical students, led and organized the transition to medical school wilderness trip, and mentored undergraduates through the Asian American Interactive Mentoring Program. Currently, James is a Pediatrics-Anesthesia resident at Harvard.

Contact James at info@crackingmedadmissions.com

ABOUT THE AUTHORS

Devin Nambiar was born and raised in the San Francisco Bay Area, and has lived around the world since finishing high school. He has been advising students at the high school and college levels for over a decade. While doing his undergrad at Columbia University, majoring in Math, he taught high school students from the Bronx the principles of entrepreneurship as the co-founder of Columbia Students in Free Enterprise. After graduating, he founded a college admissions consultancy in his hometown and spent a year helping local high school students gain entry to their top choice schools. He then worked in test prep and mobile learning technologies for two years in Seoul, South Korea before coming back to California to work in tech. He is an evangelist for healthcare technology, and recognizes that potential doctors have to affect change not just at the operating table, but in the business world as well. In his day job, he is currently Head of Product Management for Asia-Pacific at Electronic Arts, and travels the world working with game development teams from across the company. Devin is a member of the Forbes Technology Council, PocketGamer's Mobile Mavens, and is both an active voice in the industry and an author on technology and business. He currently resides in Shanghai. He continues to consult for college and graduate school admissions, and he is active in the Columbia Shanghai Alumni Council and an interviewer for prospective Columbia applicants. Contact Devin at info@crackingmedadmissions.com

PREFACE

Rachel, Rishi, James, and Devin have advised pre-meds with thousands of applications. Now, we want to help you! We know the ins and outs of the admissions process. We sit on interview panels and selection committees for medical schools, universities, and competitive scholarships.

So what's unique about this book? First, we took the most common questions that pre-meds have asked us and offered our expertise in an easy-to-read Question & Answer format. We were frustrated as pre-meds with the overly general advice we received from other resources, so we filled this book with specific examples and answers. For instance, if you want to see sample thank-you letters or interview questions, this book has all the information at your fingertips. Second, some application questions don't have one correct answer. In these cases, we contribute our differing perspectives to help you make informed decisions. Finally, we highlighted several other medical students' stories so you can learn from their journeys too. We have anecdotes about what people did during their time off and how to approach MD/PhD interviews. Our advisees have found the 50 successful essays included in this book to be extremely helpful.

We wish you the best of luck with the application process! This book will no doubt be invaluable to you along your journey. We are here to help every step of the way.

Sincerely,

Rachel, Rishi, James & Devin
Cracking Med School Admissions Team

CHAPTER 1. BEFORE YOU EVEN APPLY...

There are thousands of medical school applicants, so your job is to present your application in a way that highlights why you are unique. In order to be a competitive applicant, your application should be strong in the following three components:

First, you need to have a high enough GPA and MCAT scores. The bottom line is that your scores are an indicator to medical schools that you can handle the rigorous coursework. And make no mistake, the coursework in medical school is TOUGH. What if you did not do well in certain science classes and your GPA isn't as high as you wanted? Then do well on your MCATs and show medical schools that you can excel in medical school. Although your scores do not tell medical schools why you are unique, they do tell them that you are capable of doing well in medical school. Don't give medical schools reasons to doubt you can handle the coursework!

Second, demonstrate that you are committed to your passions. You don't have to limit your passions to science and healthcare. If you are passionate about service, global health, hard sciences, travelling, writing, acting, or dance, then that should come across in your application. Passionate people have rich experiences that are applicable to medicine. Medical schools want to see what drives you.

Third, convey to medical schools that you are a multi-dimensional person who has talents and interests outside of medicine. At the end of the day, patients want doctors who are not machines and are capable of supporting them emotionally through difficult times. Patients want their doctors to know how to care for them as a whole person, not just as a complex collection of cells. Medical schools will teach you the pathology of diseases and train you in the art of medicine. Highlighting your softer skills and your talents will signal to medical schools that you are prepared to navigate the doctor-patient relationship.

In this chapter, we answer the most common questions we have received from pre-med students who are debating whether they should apply to medical school.

If you have additional questions, feel free to contact the **Cracking Med School Admissions** *team at* **info@crackingmedadmissions.com.**

SHOULD I RETAKE MY MCAT?

Rachel: I generally advise people to retake their MCAT only under certain conditions:
1. Your score is really low and you will get screened out of the applicant pool.
2. You always scored higher on your practice tests and you are sure that you can score better if you retake the exam.
3. You think you can score at least 5 points higher.

James: If your score falls within the middle 50% of a school you are interested in applying to (check the MSAR - Medical School Admission Requirements publication for these statistics – available at: https://www.aamc.org/students/applying/requirements/msar/), I personally would not retake the MCAT. This means that you are scoring around the average of the students being admitted – although it never hurts to be above this average. It takes a lot of additional time, money, and effort that could be better spent developing your application as a whole. The MCAT is only one component of your admissions profile, and admissions committees recognize this fact.

Rishi: Deciding to retake your MCAT can be a difficult decision. When friends ask me if they should retake their MCATs, I give them the following questions to ask themselves:

1. How competitive is your MCAT score for the schools you want to attend? You can find the average MCAT score for each school at the US News & World Report site and the Medical School Admissions Requirements book as James mentioned above.
2. Is your score consistent with your grades in your science classes?
3. How much time did you spending while studying for the MCAT?
4. What was going on in your life while you were studying for the MCAT? Were you busy taking a full load of classes, volunteering with several organizations, and doing research?
5. Did you try your best? If you believe that you studied as hard as you could and consulted all resources that were available to you, then don't spend your time retaking the MCAT test.

WHEN IS THE LATEST TIME I CAN RETAKE MY MCAT?

It usually takes one month for schools to receive your official MCAT score. So if you are aiming to turn in your primary application by late July of the year you are beginning to apply (which we advise doing), then the latest time you should plan on taking your MCAT is late June.

SHOULD I TAKE TIME BETWEEN COLLEGE AND MEDICAL SCHOOL?

James: When deciding whether to take time off between undergraduate and medical school, I definitely considered other options including taking time to travel, working in a non-medicine related field, and continuing to do research. At the end of the day, nothing excited me more than the prospect of going to medical school. Therefore, if you are ready to go straight to medical school, it is absolutely appropriate to do so if you feel that your application is competitive enough to apply. Some advisors may suggest taking a year to bolster your application if your GPA/MCAT score may not be the most competitive or your application could benefit from additional experiences demonstrating your passion and interest in medicine. It is important to consider what other options are out there so that when you do start medical school, you aren't left wondering "What if I had done... X?" Moreover, depending on the school, you may have the option of deferring admission if a compelling opportunity comes up.

Rishi and Rachel: We strongly recommend taking time off between college and medical school. Medical schools aren't going anywhere, but you have the world to explore! We suggest that you do something that excites you and showcases your talents. Not only will you be a more mature applicant but also will you have more experiences to contribute as a medical student.

To give you perspective on what you can do when you take gap years, here are some profiles of what our friends did during their time before medical school:

Clinical Research – Brindha Bavan

What did you do in your year(s) between college and medical school?

During my gap year between graduating from college and entering medical school, I worked for the Department of Radiation Oncology at the Stanford Cancer Institute as a Clinical Research Coordinator. I was responsible for managing chemoradiation trials for head and neck cancer patients, and had the opportunity to spend time both advocating for patients in clinic while pursuing retrospective treatment outcomes research as well. I also definitely made it a point to take time to relax before starting medical school, so I spent one month enjoying Los Angeles with my family and traveled a bit too.

What did you gain from this experience?

While regulatory paperwork was a very effective way to thoroughly learn about the process of running a clinical trial from beginning to end, I was most grateful for my direct patient encounters. I gained immense perspective while celebrating those individuals overcoming Stage III malignancies, but also while sympathizing with others learning of metastatic disease that could only be mitigated with palliative care. The position was eye-opening as I constantly interacted with medical staff at every level - from attending physicians to residents in training to dieticians. I learned to be adaptive to diverse personalities and gain confidence in my contributions within the medical setting even this early on in my career. From a practical standpoint, I was also given opportunities to work on publications, which encouraged me to hone my knowledge of statistics and scientific writing skills. Overall, I feel fortunate to have these experiences to call upon as I continue through my medical education, because they remind me while there are challenging, it is all well worth it.

What advice do you have for people who are taking time before medical school and doing something similar to what you did?

I am a huge proponent of taking time off. I really believe that it enables you to challenge yourself in new ways and mature your perspective. Whether you decide to work in industry, backpack through Europe, brave the world of finance, help your family's business, or follow the more traditional path with research, community health, or international relief work, you are preparing yourself to bring more to the table as a medical school applicant. Whatever you choose to do, it is very likely that you will strengthen your skills in leadership, public-speaking, problem-solving, team-building, advocacy, etc. – all of which apply to medicine.

Other thoughts:

This time can also allow those who are not sure about whether medicine is right for you to get your feet wet in healthcare and address your concerns before jumping in. There are financial benefits if you choose to work during this time as well, since money saved can be applied toward the cost of medical school or personal expenses such as travel. I have quite a few friends who went right through to medical school from undergrad and are very happy with their decisions, but I also have yet to meet someone who has regretted taking time off due to the thoughtful insight it granted them.

Clinical Research – Alexa Glencer

What did you do in your year(s) between college and medical school?

After graduating from college, I spent a year working as a premedical intern at UCSF's Breast Care Center. In this capacity, I was granted the opportunity to become involved in active clinical trial design, implementation, and analysis in the field of breast oncology. I served as the clinical coordinator for a metastatic tissue banking study and for two trials designed to assess the safety and efficacy of scalp-cooling devices intended to prevent chemotherapy-induced alopecia. I worked closely with my principal investigators (PIs), who became my faculty mentors, and interacted daily with patients being seen in clinic, receiving infusions, and undergoing surgery or other invasive procedures.

What did you gain from this experience?

I cannot overemphasize how valuable this experience was in reaffirming my desire to pursue a career in medicine, in identifying a specific subspecialty area that I find enthralling, and in providing me with an environment that dramatically facilitated my personal development. I learned a tremendous amount about the fields of breast medical oncology, surgery, and even radiation oncology in the context of practice within a vibrant academic medical center. My faculty mentors have become lifelong role models, and my patients, with whom I shared such genuine and profound experiences, imparted wisdom and true inspiration.

What advice do you have for people who are taking time before medical school and doing something similar to what you did?

It is critical that you possess a strong independent work ethic and that you take care to balance efficiency with impromptu learning opportunities. Allow yourself time to gain an understanding of the particular culture of your working environment and then work within the system. There will inevitably come times when you are frustrated, exhausted, and feel underappreciated; this sensation is representative of real-world adversity. The time spent away from formal academic training will prove invaluable in developing a better understanding of yourself, a sense of what you would like to achieve, and, most importantly, of what is required to elicit meaning and purpose from your future occupation.

Global Health and Masters Programs – Rishi Mediratta

I took three years off between college and medical school. After college, I interned for the World Health Organization in Geneva for two months and then moved to Ethiopia to implement several child health projects. Specifically, I conducted a community survey of child health practices with the Ethiopian Ministry of Health, was a consultant to the World Bank about Ethiopia's national nutrition program, and launched a community-based health and education program in one village for vulnerable children.

After Ethiopia, I lived in London for two years as a British Marshall Scholar where I completed a Masters in public health at the London School of Hygiene and Tropical Medicine and a Masters in medical anthropology at the School of Oriental and African Studies. I have my whole life to be a doctor and am glad that I had the opportunity to learn more about different cultures, learn more about the world, and learn more about myself.

By studying medical anthropology, I learned more about explanatory concepts of health and illness among Ethiopian adolescents. I was able to apply a theoretical understanding of medical anthropology issues to the field to reveal insights about how to design and implement health programs for the youth. Additionally, I loved studying at London School of Hygiene & Tropical Medicine because my peers were warm, my professors were accessible, and the environment was collegial. Returning to public health after training in medical anthropology was a stimulating experience because I was able to consider the unintended consequences and social implications of public health interventions.

Global Health – Rachel Rizal

I spent a year after graduation in the Philippines on a Fulbright fellowship because I wanted to learn more about healthcare in a developing country. I was able to apply what I had learned in college about infectious diseases and immunization programs to my work in the Philippines. By working in community health centers, I was able to gain clinical experience by serving the poorest people.

I had three main projects in the Philippines and gained different skills from each project:

1. World Health Organization - We aimed to improve Hepatitis B vaccination rates among newborns. In order to accomplish this, we worked with city governments, local hospitals, and community health centers. We forged partnerships so that private hospitals (where mothers gave birth) would send newborns to the community health centers for free vaccines. I learned how to negotiate and create strong partnerships between the public and private sectors.

2. HIV awareness campaign - The HIV epidemic was only beginning when I lived in the Philippines. I worked with an infectious disease doctor to educate Filipinos about the disease. We organized a rock concert, created a television commercial, and spoke with numerous journalists. It was my first time working on a nation-wide public health program.

3. Cervical cancer research - I worked at the national Philippine Cancer Institute and collected data on the disease burden of cervical cancer among Filipino women. We used this information to justify that the national government should help fund HPV vaccines as part of its immunization program.

Private Sector, Healthcare Consulting –
Rachel Rizal

I spent another year in between college and medical school working for a healthcare consulting firm that advised biotech/pharmaceutical companies about business practices.

For example, I was on a team that collected prescribing data from oncologists. We then used this information to advise a pharmaceutical company on its cancer drug's marketing strategy. In another project, I advised a pharmaceutical company on how to improve its drug distribution channels. I enjoyed my time working for a healthcare consulting company because I learned a lot about the science behind the projects, but was able to see these scientific issues through a business lens.

Additionally, working in a corporate environment taught me managerial skills that I can apply to clinics and my future jobs. At one point, I was working with four different managers and had to juggle their various working styles. I foresee myself working with different types of people in medicine, and I believe the corporate world was a good experience for learning how to be an effective leader within teams.

Non-traditional Applicant, Post
Baccalaureate, Musician – Ben Robinson

His Story: Ben spent 12 years after college as a violinist, composer, producer, and director. He has a doctorate of musical arts in which he focused on multi-media stage performance linking visual arts to music. He also has a nonprofit stage company dedicated to the same goal. The tragic events of 9/11 took place while he was pursing his doctorate and inspired him to create the Musician's Alliance for Peace (MAP) as a mechanism to inspire alternatives to war. Through MAP, Ben created the yearly Music for Peace Project (2004-2009) which coordinated over 400 charity concerts worldwide.

He found his work as an artist and organizer fulfilling but as a hands-on person, he wanted to help others more concretely. He first tested his interest in medicine by becoming certified and volunteering as an Emergency Medical Technician in New York.

Soon thereafter, Ben enrolled in Columbia University's Post baccalaureate Premedical Program. There, he had access to Columbia's medical faculty and worked as a videographer in the surgery department to make educational videos for residents. Simultaneously, Ben won a MacArthur prize to work on developing online tools to make news actionable.

Now, Ben is a student at Stanford School of Medicine where he has a new start-up and is focused on utilizing his background in teaching to support innovations in learning and medical education. He still plays the violin (semi)regularly and may one day create a multi-media piece to highlight emotional, ethical and cultural currents in medicine.

HOW DO I LEARN ABOUT EACH SCHOOL?

We always encourage our advisees to speak with current students and to visit each school. However, if that's not possible, there are a plethora of other resources to learn more about a medical school:
- Website: good for an overview of the different programs available and general information about the curriculum
- Current students: learn about specific opportunities available and what it's like to really be a student at that medical school
- Doctors: learn about different specialties and the patient population they serve
- Advisors: can give you specific information about programs and the curriculum
- Your school's pre-med office: good at giving you more general information about each school

HOW DO I SELECT WHERE I SHOULD APPLY?

James: Only apply to schools that you can actually see yourself going to. The admissions process is time consuming and expensive. There are multiple dimensions by which to stratify schools, however the way I did it was by geography. With each school I selected, I thought carefully about the realities of living in that particular location. Giving consideration to non-academic factors such as proximity to family/significant-others/friends is also part of the decision process. Going solely by school reputation can often lead to applying for schools one might not ever truly like to attend. Each school has a personality that needs to fit with yours.

Rishi: I came up with a list of schools where I wanted to attend and categorized them as "reach schools," "schools where I am competitive," and "safety schools." My school preferences were based on location, culture, curriculum, program, faculty members with similar research interests, and students' perceived happiness. I applied to medical school when I was living in Ethiopia, so I limited my list of schools to those I really wanted to attend and would fly back for the opportunity to interview at.

HOW MUCH TIME SHOULD I BE ALLOCATING TO COMPLETING THE APPLICATION?

Rachel: I spent the most time on my AMCAS application. It took me 2-3 weeks to write my primary statement and finish my AMCAS. I have had friends who worked on their applications full-time and finished everything within a month. I spent another two months while I was working a full-time job to complete my secondaries.

Rishi: I considered writing my primary and secondary applications as a job. I set aside protected time to work on my application. Starting the spring before the beginning of the cycle, I began reflecting upon my clinical volunteering and research opportunities. I kept a running document about the experiences that shaped why I wanted to be a doctor. As I thought about my clinical experiences, I wished I had kept a journal so I could draw from the specific conversations that I had with patients. After I submitted my primary application, I spent a great deal of time completing each school's secondary application, which all had different prompts and varying word counts. If you are in school or working, plan to carve out time to work on your application.

Also, I recommend spending time before the application cycle to reflect on your experiences and how they connect with one another. The more you know about why you want to be a doctor and how your experiences demonstrate this, the smoother the application process will be.

James: If you are doing something else while applying for medical school (e.g. senior year of undergraduate, full time job/research, etc.), it is very important to set aside dedicated time to work on your applications. Even before secondary applications are sent out, you can look up secondary questions from years past and begin drafting secondary essays. Be mindful of how long it takes for you to write and edit as the number of essays can pile up quickly. Some secondary applications carry deadlines, while others are read on a rolling basis. Either way, it is to your advantage to have enough time in your week to continuously work on your application. For me, this was upwards of 10 hours per week while still being a full-time student.

How do I take the US News and World Report ranking into account when selecting a school?

Rishi: The *US News and World Report* ranking list is only one metric used to rank medical schools. The ranking is heavily based on National Institutes of Health research dollars, which does not directly translate into quality of medical education.

The *US News and World Report* rankings did not help me appreciate the differences in each school's mission and philosophy of education nor the extent to which resources and opportunities are available to medical students. Instead of relying on the *US News and World Report*'s list to decide where you should go to medical school, make your own list of what you want in a medical school and rank how each school satisfies your needs.

James: It can often be difficult to completely disregard the weight of the *US News and World Ranking* reports on medical schools. However, in considering what medical center is the best for medical students, it does a very poor job. When I applied, I did not know many people who were already attending medical schools. Therefore, I relied heavily upon getting to know students during interview days in order to gauge the personality and fit I had with each school. This was far more important than the numerical rank of a school.

SHOULD I APPLY MD/PHD:

We asked our MD/PhD friends about their perspectives and advice for applying to MD/PhD programs:

Spotlight on MD/PhD Applicants

Spotlight on Gerald Tiu

Medical School: Stanford

---

1. Why did you decide to pursue an MD/PhD?

I chose to pursue an MD/PhD because I believe medical training and graduate training can benefit one another.

First of all, I love science and research and I think that is a prerequisite to do graduate training. Basic science and research can definitely contribute knowledge to the medical field and can occasionally lead to translational discoveries that directly impact patients. Although a PhD is not technically necessary for strong research training, it definitely is an avenue to really learn the foundations of science and to maybe one day apply them to medical problems. PhD training also teaches perseverance, creative thinking, and an ability to develop practical solutions for difficult problems, a set of skills that would be helpful in the clinic.

One of the most awesome aspects of doing dual training, however, is how having clinical (and even preclinical medical training) experience, which allows you to have a real organic, broad, yet very in-depth perspective on human biology and disease. This perspective is an attribute that most graduate students, post-docs, and pure research faculty never really get to experience. They understand in-depth their own very narrow field of expertise, but they are not trained to see broad connections as relevant to human biology. With medical training, you really get to see links between different biological processes and disease, and form hypotheses that are more relevant to clinical problems. In addition, in medicine (and even in preclinical training), you don't choose the patients that come to you nor do you choose the classes that are required in the medical curriculum. You end up seeing things and learning things from patients, colleagues, and classes that go beyond your normal field of expertise and comfort zone. In a way, diverse patients and the broad medical school curriculum present hypotheses to you that you wouldn't normally think of. If a patient comes in with strange and unexplained symptoms, that encounter could become a research question that you may be able to probe through your research but that may not have been evident had you not met the patient.

Lastly, working with patients is awesome and it is refreshing to be motivated by patient encounters and conversations. At least for me, patient encounters always motivate and remind me of why I am pursuing my dual medical and research degree.

2. How were MD/PhD applications different than MD applications?

The MD/PhD applications differ from MD applications in that they are more heavily research focused. It becomes more of a prerequisite to have a strong research background in order to apply to an MD/PhD program. Letters of recommendations from principal investigators are also important along with a research background in which you have worked to develop a scientific story, ideally from beginning to end.

3. What was your experience filling out MD/PhD applications?

Filling out my MD/PhD applications were challenging, but they were also great in that they gave me an opportunity to think deeply about why I wanted to pursue an MD/PhD degree, to truly reflect on and understand my research, and to construct a narrative that brings together all my research in medicine and science into one story.

4. Any tips for applications?

Know your research and your general research field well. Many of the interviews are research focused and it is important that you understand why your research is significant. Spend some time reading primary literature when you can, especially on topics related to your research and research interests. I think, most importantly, show that you are enthusiastic about continuing a research career and show that you have a research background that supports that enthusiasm.

You will often be asked why both an MD and PhD. There are many answers for this, many of them are cliché, but as long as you are enthusiastic, honest, and well-informed regarding your answer, your answer should be okay. It also helps finding a physician-scientist role model that you can talk to and get advice from. Many schools will want to make sure you understand what matriculating into an MD/PhD program actually entails, and by having a role model, it shows that you have done your homework regarding understanding what doing a dual degree is like.

Most importantly, be yourself! Show off any quirks or special interests if you have any.

Spotlight on Daniel Kim

Medical School: Stanford

---

1. Why did you decide to do MD/PhD?

I came from more of a research background. As such, I was initially considering whether I should do a PhD or an MD/PhD. I had done some shadowing and volunteering, and those experiences convinced me that I did wanted to be involved in the clinics, not just on the research side of things, and so I applied for an MD/PhD. I believe there is a value to doing both research and clinical work, and that the two can provide interesting synergies that can drive both clinical practice and research forward.

2. How were MD/PhD applications different than MD applications?

MD/PhD applications are basically MD applications, but with extra essays and a few extra questions. You still go through AMCAS and apply as if you were an MD candidate, but each school may ask you for a different set of essays, or they may ask for the MD essays plus one or two others. Most schools also have a requirement for at least one research-oriented recommendation. In general, MD/PhD applications want to see that you have research experience and know what you are getting into by applying for eight years of school.

3. Any tips for applications?

If I would give any tips for applications, I would say the key is to have a strong research background. This should be evident in your extracurricular activities (with or without publications) and your letters of recommendation. You should also show that you have thought about what your career might look like, in terms of balancing research and clinics. Thinking about how your role models have shown that balanced research and clinics is a good way to reflect upon this. Medical schools want you to think long term and to have some idea of where you are aiming to be, even if that may change.

BEFORE YOU EVEN APPLY TO-DO LIST:

- ☐ Reflect on why you want to go to medical school
- ☐ Complete your MCAT exam
- ☐ Explore opportunities to take time before starting medical school
- ☐ Decide whether you want to apply MD or MD/PhD
- ☐ Decide what qualities you want in a medical school and finalize a list of schools to apply to
- ☐ Protect time to complete the application process

If you have any additional questions, feel free to contact the *Cracking Med School Admissions* team at **info@crackingmedadmissions.com.**

Chapter 2. Primary Applications

"Moments and people. Moments and People. When you think about your activities, think about the moments and the people." My mentor recited these words to me as if they were a jingle. This piece of advice has stuck with me after numerous applications, and it has been the advice I've passed on to my friends.

So how does filling out your medical school applications work in practice? This chapter gives our tidbits of advice, and the process we go through in order to fill out our medical school applications. The American Medical College Application Service, or AMCAS for short, is the online form for applicants to fill in their primary applications and designate which medical schools to send their applications to.

If you have additional questions or need help with essays, feel free to contact the Cracking Med School Admissions *team at* **info@crackingmedadmissions.com.**

FILLING OUT THE AMCAS

What can I do prior to filling out the AMCAS to help me fill out the application?

We believe that a systematic way to think about your activities is a great way to fill out both the "activities" section and to generate ideas for your essays. Here is the step-wise process we recommend:

Step-wise approach to brainstorming the AMCAS application

1. **Activities:** Write down all the activities you have participated in -- this can be anything from running to conducting research to working a full-time job
2. **Positions:** List all positions and leadership offices held

3. **Skills:** List the skills you have learned from each activity
4. **Impact:** What impact did you have? If you can quantify the impact that would be best (e.g. Educated 6,000 elementary school students about diarrheal diseases)
5. **Inspirational Moments:** Write about an inspirational moment or person. Reflect on times you had that "Aha!" moment, or a time you have had an inspiring conversation with a mentor or patient

Remember, this is just a brainstorm... so don't stress out and have fun reflecting on all your accomplishments!

We wanted to give you a couple of examples of how we have used our step-wise process to achieve success.

Example 1. Breast Cancer Chemotherapy Clinical Trial Researcher
Positions: Research Assistant
Skills: - Interviewed patients about their experiences with chemotherapy
- Tracked cancer progression during a 1-, 3-, and 6-month follow-up.
- Enrolled patients into study and explained research trial to them
Impact: Enrolled 100 patients into the clinical trial over a period of 6 months
Inspirational Moments: I got to know the patients at the cancer center outside of patient enrollment: Mrs. Liu was an immigrant from Taiwan. Her husband had died from colon cancer a few years ago. She had no family in the area so I kept her company and chatted with her throughout her chemotherapy. I learned about her life story and her reflections as a patient suffering from cancer.

Example 2. Running Club
Positions: President - Senior year / Treasurer - Junior year
Skills: - Treasurer - Learned how to manage a $10,000 budget for an organization
- President - First time managing a 40-person organization
Impact: Organized first 5k/10k benefit run to raise money for the American Cancer Society
- Raised $10,000 in sponsorships from local restaurants and school fundraisers
Inspirational Moments: - The running club had people with a wide range of experience and interest in running. There were the hardcore runners who ran marathons and then there were members who ran for recreation. There was a girl in the running club named Anika. While she loved running, she had never run a marathon before. I encouraged her to sign-up for a marathon, created a practice schedule, and trained with her. When I watched her finish her marathon, I was so happy that she did it! This was the first time I was able to use my experience and my encouragement to push somebody to go beyond what they believed were their limits.

IN WHAT FORMAT SHOULD I WRITE ABOUT MY ACTIVITIES ON MY APPLICATION?

The big debate here is whether you should write your activity descriptions in paragraph form or bullet form.

Rishi: I considered each AMCAS entry to be a mini story about my experiences. The story format allowed me to connect different experiences together, which I thought was beneficial. Here's an example of how I provided details about one experience in a story format:

Hospice Volunteer | Kalamazoo, MI

"Heartland Hospice provides palliative and supportive services for individuals in the final phases of terminal illnesses. It strives to meet the physical, psychological, social, and spiritual needs of clients and their

caregivers. My role as a volunteer was to be a friendly visitor and companion to the terminally ill. After completing a basic hospice education course, I was assigned a few clients to visit in different nursing homes every week for the summer. I documented my general impressions of the clients and any changes in their mental and physical status, comments which were then added to each client's medical file. My most memorable client was Mrs. S, a 79-year old woman who had just suffered a stroke. She was unable to talk coherently, but this did not stop us from communicating. I asked her yes/no questions and she would nod in response. It made my day when I was able to make her laugh or chuckle, or even just put her hand on mine. I learned that the end of life for individuals in hospice can be a lonely and painful process. Having someone there to break the silence can make the dying process more comfortable, and I was grateful to have had this volunteer experience."

Rachel and James: We like to cut to the chase and use the bullet point format. Use strong action verbs to delineate your contributions to projects and volunteer commitments. Example:

Health Matters | Princeton, New Jersey
- *LEADERSHIP POSITIONS: Co-Founder & President*
- *Organized and led parent and student interactive health workshops to educate minority and low-income families about various health topics such as nutrition, dentistry, and infectious diseases*
- *Recruited bi-lingual doctors to speak with parents and answer questions about healthy living*
- *Worked with a Princeton nutritionist to produce a local television show on healthy-eating and sugar*

Regardless of whether you describe your activities in a narrative format or in bullet points, using active verbs is essential. Here is a good resource for a list of commonly used verbs:

COMMUNICATION

Aided
Advised
Arbitrated
Clarified
Co-authored
Collaborated
Consulted
Coordinated
Counseled

Defined
Enlisted
Formulated
Influenced
Informed
Inspired
Interpreted
Interviewed
Mediated

Merged
Negotiated
Promoted
Publicized
Recommended
Represented
Resolved
Suggested

CREATIVE

Abstracted
Acted
Adapted
Composed
Conceptualized
Created
Designed
Developed
Directed

Drew
Fashioned
Generated
Illustrated
Imagined
Improvised
Integrated
Innovated
Painted

Performed
Planned
Problem solved
Shaped
Synthesized
Visualized
Wrote

DETAIL

Analyzed	Compiled	Processed
Approved	Documented	Recorded
Arranged	Enforced	Retrieved
Classified	Followed through	Set priorities
Collated	Met deadlines	Systemized
Compared	Prepared	Tabulated

FINANCIAL

Administered	Calculated	Managed
Allocated	Computed	Performed
Analyzed	Developed	Planned
Appraised	Evaluated	Projected
Audited	Figured	
Budgeted	Maintained	

LEADERSHIP

Administered	Expanded	Produced
Chaired	Facilitated	Recommended
Convinced	Improved	Reviewed
Directed	Initiated	Supervised
Examined	Managed	
Executed	Oversaw	

MANUAL SKILLS

Arranged	Constructed	Handled
Assembled	Controlled	Installed
Bound	Cut	Invented
Built	Designed	Maintained
Checked	Developed	Monitored
Classified	Drove	Operated

Prepared	Repaired	Tested

ORGANIZING

Achieved	Delegated	Prepared
Assigned	Developed	Prioritized
Consulted	Established	Produced
Contracted	Evaluated	Recommended
Controlled	Negotiated	Reported
Coordinated	Organized	
Decided	Planned	

RESEARCH/INVESTIGATION

Calculated	Discovered	Investigated
Cataloged	Examined	Monitored
Collected	Experimented	Proved
Computed	Extrapolated	Reviewed
Conducted	Evaluated	Surveyed
Correlated	Gathered	Tested
Critiqued	Identified	
Diagnosed	Inspected	

SERVICE

Advised	Demonstrated	Mentored
Attended	Explained	Provided
Cared	Furnished	Purchased
Coached	Generated	Referred
Coordinated	Inspected	Repaired
Counseled	Installed	Submitted
Delivered	Issued	

TEACHING

Adapted	Evaluated	Represented
Advised	Informed	Supported
Clarified	Inspired	Taught
Coached	Motivated	Trained
Developed	Participated	Verified
Encouraged	Provided	

TECHNICAL

Assembled	Engineered	Remodeled
Built	Fabricated	Repaired
Calculated	Maintained	Solved
Computed	Operated	
Designed	Programmed	

Reproduced with permission from:
http://studentaffairs.stanford.edu/cdc/resumes/verbs

TIP: Activities on a Resume

Remember to write more about what you did and what you gained from the experience rather than spending a lot of time talking about the organization

---

The AMCAS recently allowed applicants to write an extra 1,325 word description of their most significant activities. What should I do?

Like your personal statement, the descriptions of your most significant activities allow you to differentiate yourself. Treat this as an opportunity to write a short answer for each activity.

- DO: Write about how this activity / experience has motivated you to go into medicine
- DO: Elaborate on your motivation / development gained from this activity
- DON'T: Have the same essays as your secondary applications

TIP: Hours of Activity

Don't forget to include the number of hours you spend thinking, planning, and attending meetings in addition to time spent on the activity itself!

How will the information I put on the AMCAS be used?

Rachel: I was an editor for a Bioethics Journal in college. One interviewer, who I later learned was a bioethicist, asked me very direct questions: What was my favorite bioethics question? What were the different perspectives written by writers in my journal? What were my opinions on the topic? Be prepared to discuss anything you put in your application in depth.

Rishi: The AMCAS experiences are often used as starting points during medical school interviews. Interviewers will use the following question: "So, tell me why you did X?" I had many interviewers ask me to provide more details about my AMCAS experiences. Be prepared to defend everything you write in the activities section because interviewers will be looking for you to articulate the depth of your experiences.

James: The information in the AMCAS activities section will be used in a variety of ways depending on the school. In open-application interviews, your interviewers will be given a copy of your AMCAS application and oftentimes questions will be drawn from the activities that you discuss. Of course in the review process of each applicant, the AMCAS activities will help the admissions committee form a picture of who you are and what you have done. Therefore it is important to represent yourself well on the AMCAS application.

DO YOU HAVE ANY ADVICE ON HOW TO COMBINE ACTIVITIES, ESPECIALLY WHEN I'M RUNNING OUT OF SPACE?

Think about the responsibilities you have and the mission for each activity. Are there commonalities? If so, think about combining these activities because you can probably combine the descriptions.

Here are some examples:

- If you shadow at different hospitals, combine the hours and put all these experiences down as one activity
- If you teach health education for different volunteer organizations, combine these experiences into one activity
- Put all publications / posters under one activity and provide short descriptions / abstracts for each

How should I describe the awards I've won?

Be sure to include:

- How competitive the application process
- Selection criteria
- The level at which the award was given
  (international / national / state / regional / school)

When should I turn in my primaries?

Turn in primaries as early as possible. We cannot emphasize this point enough! Since applications are reviewed on a rolling basis, the timing of when you turn in your primaries can determine whether or not you get an interview. What this means is that as applications are turned in, schools are already beginning to assign their limited number of interview slots.

A rough goal should be aiming to turn in your primaries by the end of July at the latest. If you are a strong applicant, you may be able to get away with turning in your primaries during the first half of August, but there is little reason not to turn in your application sooner. With secondary applications, you should try to submit them as soon as you receive them.

TIP: Submit Application Early

Early application submission =
Higher chance of getting an interview

PERSONAL STATEMENT:

WHAT'S THE PURPOSE OF THE PERSONAL STATEMENT?

The purpose of the personal statement is to provide the admissions officer information about who you are and why you want to go to medical school. It gives your application life and personality.

We think the personal statement is a place where you can showcase yourself. It can help differentiate you from other applicants and get you an interview.

WHAT SHOULD I WRITE ABOUT?

We know that writing a personal statement can be daunting. What experiences can you write about in about a page that encapsulates your decision to pursue medicine? For starters, think about the experiences that have left you with that desire to be a doctor. Or, are there any mentors or individuals who have inspired you to pursue medicine?

Questions to ask yourself when brainstorming your personal statement:

- What am I going to do with my medical degree?
- What do I want to tell the admissions committee about myself?
- Are there any interesting stories related to medicine/healthcare that are unique to my experiences?
- What cultural experiences have I had that informed my experiences with healthcare?
- What do I want the reader to learn about me from reading my personal statement?

- Are there any skills or personality traits I want to highlight?

Ideas for topics you can write about:

- People who have inspired you to pursue medicine
- Clinical experiences and stories
- Organizations you have been involved with and the impact you have made. However, don't be redundant if you have already discussed the importance of an organization you were a part of or experience that you had in the AMCAS activities section.
- What skills you have developed in your past experiences and how you can contribute these takeaways to your classmates and to the medical school
- Aspects of healthcare and medicine that you have been interested in and how this relates to your future endeavors
- Other information you want the admissions committee to know about you that you were not able to write in your AMCAS application

SHOULD I GET PEOPLE TO EDIT MY ESSAY?

Rachel: I ask everyone to read, edit, and give me feedback on my personal statement and essays. While some of my essays are very personal, I believe that getting feedback from other readers allows me to know the impression people have of me by reading my essays. I make sure to ask a wide array of people:
- I ask individuals of different ages. Why? Perhaps somebody who is a lot older will have a different read on the essay than my peers. Also, asking older individuals helps me catch times when I use colloquial lingo or a concept that is only easily understood by younger generations.

- I ask individuals from different backgrounds: Does somebody with an economics/business background get the same impression of me than my friends who have a healthcare background? I like asking my friends who have non-science backgrounds to read my essays to make sure the language in my essays is not too technical.
- Big picture versus detailed edits: I know which friends are good at giving me feedback on big picture concepts. Some of my other friends are good at giving me suggestions on how to improve my sentence structure. Finally, a couple of my friends are excellent at proofreading – they can catch the small grammar mistakes that are hard to see after writing multiple drafts.

Rishi: I was very open about sharing my personal statement with close friends. My best friends helped me the most because they commented on whether my essay accurately reflected my experiences. Also, my school's writing center was a fantastic resource to help me better connect my ideas and to provide stylistic feedback. The staff members at the writing center have worked with hundreds of successful medical school applicants and worked with me until I was sure that my essay was unique and well-structured. I also shared my essay with a friend who was not in the health field because I wanted to ensure that the nuances to my decision for studying medicine could be understood by anyone.

James: The personal statement is personal. The people who know you best – friends and family – will be the best at helping you reflect upon the prompt at hand when it comes to your personal statement. Although the AMCAS primary is fairly flexible, the underlying question it should provide an answer to is "Why medicine?" Even if this question is answered indirectly, the personal statement should try to convey a sense for who you are as a person – what motivates you, what you care about, and why you are interested in going down the path of an MD. Mentors who have helped inspire you to pursue medicine are also a good resource in terms of finding people to provide feedback.

PRIMARY APPLICATION TO-DO LIST:

☐ Start brainstorming both the AMCAS activities and personal statement topics
☐ Write your personal statement as early as possible
☐ Use action verbs when describing your activities
☐ Edit your essay and consider sharing drafts with friends, family, mentors, and colleagues
☐ Submit your AMCAS application and send to all the schools to which you are applying

If you have additional questions or need help with essays, feel free to contact the Cracking Med School Admissions *team at* **info@crackingmedadmissions.com.**

CHAPTER 3. LETTERS OF RECOMMENDATION

It can be challenging to obtain strong recommendation letters, particularly when you are taking classes with hundreds of students and your professors may not seem interested in getting to know you. With adequate preparation and a well-crafted strategy, you will be able to build strong relationships with your teachers and mentors and obtain strong recommendation letters.

Why are recommendation letters important for admissions committees? First, a letter legitimizes your achievements and serves as external validation to your work. Second, letters provide admissions committees with insight into your character, your values, and your personality traits. You may have a strong academic record, but do you have the qualities needed to care for sick patients? Your mentors and professors will be able to give examples about you that illustrate your unique attributes that will help you become a successful physician. Third, recommendation letters provide context to your achievements. Your mentors have the liberty to brag on your behalf. If you are the only person who got the top grade in a class or you are among the brightest students that a professor has known, then a strong letter will contextualize these achievements.

Overall, we think of the medical school application as one big jigsaw puzzle, with letters of recommendation as a major portion of the big picture. Before we even ask our professors for a letter, we think about what aspect of the application they can lend credibility to and how they can give a "personal touch" to the application.

If you have additional questions, feel free to contact the Cracking Med School Admissions *team at **info@crackingmedadmissions.com.***

HOW DO YOU APPROACH GETTING RECOMMENDATION LETTERS?

Rishi: When I start getting recommendation letters, I think about the process in three components. First, I build strong relationships with my recommenders Then, I select the recommenders that will write the strongest letter. Finally, I request the letter.

Building strong relationships

In order to obtain a strong recommendation letter, plan to invest time in getting to know your recommender. There are many ways to build a strong relationship with your potential recommender. For example, pick your recommender's brain about books, articles, and current events. If there is an article that your recommender may enjoy, send it to him; actions like this let your recommender know that you are thinking of him. If your recommender teaches your class, contribute regularly in and out of class by offering your insights, demonstrating your curiosity, and describing your experiences. If you are working on an extracurricular activity that may be of interest to your recommender, ask for his opinion. Find a reason to solicit advice from your recommender. The main objective is to have your recommenders become invested in you. As long as you are genuinely interested in building a mentee-mentor relationship, you will be successful in obtaining a strong letter.

TIP: Recommenders

Identify faculty members and mentors who will invest in you. Cultivate relationships with faculty members who want to spend time with you one-on-one, develop your skills, and mentor you.

Selecting your recommenders

When an admissions committee member reads all of your letters, he should be impressed with the depth of your experiences, your strong academic record, your motivation to study medicine, and your commitment to healthcare. Select recommenders who will provide complementary perspectives about you and your work. In selecting your recommenders, you want to be seen as a well-rounded applicant, one who has a strong academic record and has excelled in many areas.

Here are potential recommenders and the perspectives they will have in your application:

1. *Your academic advisor can provide a picture about the trajectory of your academic achievements and an overall picture about your motivation to study medicine*
2. *Your research advisor can comment about the merits of your research*
3. *Your science teacher can comment about your ability to excel in the sciences*
4. *Your humanities teachers can comment on your ability to excel in the non-science areas*
5. *Your mentor can comment on your motivation to study medicine and personal experiences in medicine*
6. *Your advisor or boss can highlight your projects, work ethic, and how you have impacted an organization.*

Don't wait until a few months before you apply to medical school to ask your professors and mentors for recommendation letters. Start early! If you identify a faculty member who you want to write a letter, follow the process below to request a letter.

Requesting a letter

After you have developed a strong relationship with your potential recommender, it is essential that you plan how to obtain a strong letter. This is what I did:

1. Identify a recommender who is willing to write a strong letter for you.
2. Ask the recommender if they are willing to write a strong recommendation letter for you either in writing or in person.
3. Provide your recommenders with your resume and a copy of your medical school essay. It is important that recommenders see a draft of your essay so that

they can comment on your motivation for pursuing medicine.

4. Schedule a meeting to talk about the recommendation letter and your decision to go to medical school. Ask your recommender if they are have all the information they need to write a strong letter.
5. Give your recommenders at least 6 weeks to write the letter.
6. Write a thank you letter after the letter is complete.
7. Let your recommenders know the outcome of your application. You will be surprised how often students forget to update their letter writers.

James: When working with employers and taking classes with professors, developing a good relationship with these people will serve to provide you easy sources of recommendation letters. I often wish I had realized that I shouldn't have been as intimidated by professors/supervisors early on in college, which would have allowed me to forge closer ties with the people I worked with. Later on, I was able to create closer relationships by actively seeking my mentors out, defining a mentor-mentee relationship in which I was able to provide my knowledge and skills in exchange for wisdom and guidance, and in some cases even becoming friends. When you have a strong relationship, mentors are always happy to support your future endeavors - whether it is writing a letter or providing advice and guidance.

Rachel: I first ask my advisors if they are able to write me a GREAT letter of recommendation. Usually, I will ask to have an in-person meeting with each recommendation writer in order to discuss my application with them. During this meeting, I usually discuss the themes of my application and how they can tailor their recommendation letters to fit these themes.

Here's a sample of the document I give my recommendation writers:

Letter of Recommendation from Professor Grossman:

Overall themes of my application:
- Interested in the intersection of medicine, policy, public health, and business
- I want to use my clinical experiences and medical knowledge while practicing medicine to serve on policy committees and create partnerships with businesses and NGOs to improve healthcare globally.
- I like educating people about health.
- I feel that being a doctor is a great opportunity for me to educate individuals from all walks of life about taking care of their bodies, and I will have the ability to impact and improve people's health.

Some specifics I thought you could touch on:
Research skills and resourcefulness:
- Analyzed the strength of Los Angeles' after school programs even though there were no written sources
- I interviewed everyone at the organization, from the CEO/CFO to the volunteer coordinator. I got everyone's contact information through cold-calling.
- Analysis: Pieced together different pieces of information I gathered from the various interviews in order to come up with a holistic picture of LA's BEST - both its strengths, and weaknesses.

TIP: Recommendation Letters

Have a good combination of different types of recommendation letters! Your recommendation writers should be able to write about you from varying perspectives

---

WHO DID WE ASK FOR LETTERS OF RECOMMENDATION AND WHY?

Rachel:

Senior thesis advisor: He wrote about me in an academic context and what made my public policy research successful.

Doctor I worked with in the Philippines on an HIV Awareness Campaign: He talked about my resourcefulness and creativity to recruit a team and produce an MTV commercial for HIV awareness. My mentor also commented on my ability to work with diverse types of individuals: media, foreigners, doctors, and patients.

Education Task Force Advisor: I was part of a task force that advised the Philadelphia government on how to improve its after school programs. I was responsible for interviewing the after school programs in Los Angeles in order to learn about its best practices that could transfer to Philadelphia. My advisor was able to talk about my research and she also commented on how I worked with a team of peers.

Physics TA: My Physics TA wrote about my class participation and hard work in order to understand different physics concepts.

Rishi:

Major academic advisor: I took a class with my advisor my freshman year, so he knew me as a freshman and was able to comment on my growth as a student interested in public health. My advisor also supervised the public health journal that I co-edited and was able to comment about my leadership abilities.

An anthropology graduate student: I took three different anthropology classes with one graduate student whose classes convinced me to minor in anthropology.

An anthropology professor: I took two classes with a professor who specialized in African studies. He became familiar with my public health work in Ethiopia. The professor validated my interest in the socio-cultural understandings of health and healthcare.

My research advisor: I conducted my own public health study, so my advisor was able to give examples about my research abilities and dedication to healthcare.

My mentor in Ethiopia: I did a lot of shadowing and volunteer work in Ethiopia, and my mentor commented on my personal qualities and commitment to healthcare.

James:

Overall, I requested more letters (seven in total) than most schools would allow me to send. I felt that certain letter writers could better address particular areas of my application that I wanted to highlight differently for each of the schools that I was applying to.

Health policy professor: During my junior year, I took a small seminar class on health policy and development. Because the class was small, I was able to share my interest in medicine with my professor and she was very supportive of my plans to apply to medical school.

Minority health professor: This recommendation was also from a small seminar class that focused on minority health issues. In the class, I connected my background in computer science with ways to help end health disparities, which my professor was able to elaborate on in his letter.

Visiting Scholar preceptor: As a visiting scholar at the Department of Health and Human Services, I was under the direct supervision and mentorship of my team's lead – she was able to get to know me through my work and write about my motivations for entering the field of healthcare.

Software engineering employer: I asked the director of the software development group who I worked at for three years for a recommendation because he was able to highlight my dedication and commitment to online education programs.

Human physiology class professor: Human Physiology was one of my largest classes, with more than 300 students. Despite this, the professor had a lot of experience with writing medical school recommendation letters. He requested copies of my application packet and asked for a list of experiences that I felt were important to my application.

Volunteering, Assistant Dean: After volunteering for three consecutive years with organizing freshmen orientation, I had developed a good relationship with the Assistant Dean of Freshmen. She was able to comment on my work ethic and team leadership skills.
Research advisor: I asked my research advisor of 2.5 years to write a letter based on the clinical research I did with him.

After receiving an interview at Stanford, I requested two additional recommendation letters from my senior honors thesis advisors. Some schools will allow you to send in additional letters / update letters during the application cycle if you get an interview.

Public service scholars program professor: As part of my senior honors thesis project, I participated in a program that sought to develop stronger ties with community partners in order to apply the research we were each doing in a practical manner.

Honors thesis advisor: One of my honors thesis advisors was a pediatrician and he was able to further highlight how my thesis project tied together my interests in medicine and technology.

WHAT IS A COMMITTEE LETTER, AND SHOULD I USE ONE?

Some schools provide pre-med students with the option of having a committee letter. A committee letter, which is written by a faculty member or a pre-med advisor at your school, summarizes the comments from your recommendation letters. If your school will write a committee letter for you, take advantage of this opportunity because it provides an overarching context to your letters and links your experiences together. From the perspective of interviewers and admissions committees, a committee letter provides an efficient and comprehensive picture about your strengths. Additionally, the committee letter can help contextualize any extenuating circumstances that may have affected your academic performance. The downside to using a committee letter is that your individual recommendation letters have to be completed very early, usually the spring before your applications are due.

Each school will have its own process for writing committee letters. Generally, one faculty member will be assigned to your file, interview you, and be responsible for drafting your committee letter. Make sure you are aware of your school's committee letter deadlines and ensure that your individual recommendation letters are written before the school's deadline.

How do I know if my recommender will write me a good letter?

ASK directly! It never hurts to ask whether your recommender feels he/she will be able to write you a GREAT letter. Again, a strong recommendation letter is linked to having a close relationship with your mentor. Strong recommendation letters provide detailed examples about why you are an outstanding student. They touch upon your intellectual curiosity, character, and work ethic. For example, Professor X can write about how you came prepared every day to class, how you shaped the discussions with your peers, the afternoon chats you had with him during office hours, and that he selected you to be his TA the following year. Strong letters also contain specific examples. A mentor who is close to you will have ample opportunities to write about, and the reader will be able to understand your character and what drives you.

What if the professor I am asking a recommendation letter from teaches 400 people in a class?

Rachel: Even in classes with are more than 100 students, it is definitely possible to get a great letter of recommendation from the professor or TA (Teaching Assistant). Most classes that are big in size usually have TAs for each smaller section. For example, my Physics 101 class had more than 100 students enrolled and there were smaller class sections of about 15-20 students each. Since physics was not my forte, I would oftentimes go to the TA's office hours and work through difficult physics problems with him. During the weeks when there were no exams, my TA's office hours were empty and I was able to get to know him outside of the context of physics.

TIP: Teaching Assistants

It is OKAY to ask Teaching Assistants (even if they are graduate students) for letters of recommendation. Sometimes these people can talk about your involvement in a class in more detail.

ANY OTHER TIPS FOR LETTERS OF RECOMMENDATION?

Here are some other tips to keep in the back of your mind:

- Ask your recommender how often you should remind them about your letter of recommendation

Rachel: I have had professors tell me that they want an email reminder to write my recommendation every other day. I have had other professors who told me that they will finish the recommendation letter the same week and will email me once they have submitted it. I found it really helpful to ask professors if they wanted email reminders and how frequently they wanted them.

- Send thank you letters to your professors. Or better yet, send them gifts!
- Be sure to come full circle and let your recommendation writers know which schools you got rejected to, waitlisted, or got accepted. Some professors can write you a letter of support if you are waitlisted into a school. While gifts are not a requirement, showing your appreciation by updating your letter writers is a basic courtesy.

Remember, you may ask these same people for recommendations in the future.

RECOMMENDATION TO-DO LIST:

- ☐ Build strong personal relationships with people you work with
- ☐ Ask for recommendation letters well in advance
- ☐ Prepare a packet of your major themes and topics you hope the letter writer will highlight
- ☐ If your school has a letter collection service, provide your recommender with the details to send the letters
- ☐ If your school does not have a letter collection service, provide your recommenders with stamped envelopes, links to online forms, and addresses for every school
- ☐ Ask your recommenders how often they want to be reminded to complete the letter
- ☐ Confirm that your recommendation letters have been received by each school
- ☐ Write a thank you letter to all recommenders and update them about the final outcome

If you have additional questions, feel free to contact the Cracking Med School Admissions *team at* **info@crackingmedadmissions.com.**

Chapter 4. Secondaries

Secondary applications are school-specific applications that oftentimes ask you to answer questions tailored to the school. Secondaries often ask you specific questions that are not found in the primary application. Use the secondary application as a way to write about experiences that were not discussed in the primary application.

Some schools immediately send secondary applications as soon as your primary AMCAS application is processed. Some schools automatically give you a secondary if your GPA and MCAT scores are above a certain threshold level. Other schools screen your primary application first and offer secondaries to certain applicants. Don't be worried if it takes a while for your secondaries to come!

If you have additional questions or need help with essays, feel free to contact the Cracking Med School Admissions *team at* **info@crackingmedadmissions.com.**

Can I work on secondaries before I receive them?

Yes! If you have time, you can prepare secondary applications before you receive them. Schools tend to not change their secondary applications, so look online or contact the admissions office to find out what the secondary application essays will be.

When should I expect secondaries?

Some schools automatically send secondary applications immediately, while other schools have a screening process and may send qualified applicants the applications one month after your submit the AMCAS.

HOW LONG SHOULD I SPEND ON SECONDARY APPLICATIONS?

Rishi: You should aim to turn around secondary applications within one week of receiving them if you are working on the secondaries full-time. After you receive secondary applications, prioritize the secondary applications for medical schools that you are extremely interested in attending. Schools have different deadlines for secondaries, so you don't want to wait until the last day. Some schools receive applications on a rolling basis, meaning the earlier you turn in your secondaries, the better chance you have for receiving an interview.

Other tips: Remember, the more schools you apply to, the more secondary applications you will receive, and the more time you will need to spend on secondaries. Be sure to allocate time in your schedule to completing the applications. Focus on the quality of your secondary applications rather than the quantity.

Rachel: I was working a full-time job while writing my secondaries. I could have postponed my job's start date for another month or two, but I decided to write my secondaries while I was working because I am the type of person who likes to put aside my essay drafts for at least a couple of days before editing them. I actively got into a rhythm: work during the day, essays at nights and weekends.

Here's how I did it:

- Because it takes me awhile to write longer essays, I usually worked on the longer essays during the weekends.
- I wrote my shorter essays on the train ride home and if I had any other time in the evenings.
- If I had down time at work, I would edit essays or help my friends out with their applications.
- What I really recommend is working with a friend! I worked closely on my medical school applications with a good friend from high school and we held each other accountable and kept each other motivated. We would brainstorm together and edit each others' essays back and forth.

CAN I REUSE MY SECONDARY ESSAYS FOR OTHER SCHOOLS?

Some schools have similar secondary essay prompts. However, you should answer the specific prompt and follow the word count guidelines of each schools. If you reuse secondary essays, be sure to change the name of the school to which you are applying and tailor the secondary to the specific school. How? Provide specific reasons for why each medical school is a good fit for you. Are there specific professors who match your research interests? Is there an awesome pre-clinical or clinical program that interests you? Why does the school's mission statement and culture resonate with you?

DO YOU HAVE ANY TIPS FOR THE QUESTION "WHY OUR SCHOOL?"

After selecting a school to apply to, one of the most common secondary questions asked is a variation of "Why our school?" Even if not asked directly, this is often the underlying question of many secondary applications. This question is both an opportunity for the school to assess how well you know its program and offerings, as well as another opportunity for you as the applicant to reiterate and weave together your unique experiences and interests to show schools how you are a good fit with them.

For example, in recent years, Stanford has asked about what Scholarly Concentration you might be interested in (the Scholarly Concentration is a unique academic program that provides students with coursework and research in a variety of different fields). To answer this question effectively, you need to know what each of these concentrations offers, how the concentration that you choose aligns with your experience, and in turn how it will advance your education as a future physician. As mentioned before, the best way to get to find answers to these questions is to ask current students at these schools.

SECONDARY APPLICATION TO-DO LIST:

☐ Check secondary application deadlines for each school
☐ When you receive secondaries, make deadlines for yourself about when you will complete them
☐ Research each school and look for professors, activities, and programs that complement your previous experiences and interests
☐ Proofread essays that you are adapting for various schools
☐ Submit your secondaries early!

If you have additional questions or need help with essays, feel free to contact the Cracking Med School Admissions *team at* **info@crackingmedadmissions.com.**

Chapter 5: Interviews

Our team has done a multitude of interviews. We have done interviews while working abroad and during a full-time job. We have experienced tough interview questions, and we have had several interview formats (group, multiple mini interviews, one-on-one).

We have helped several of our friends with their interviews. Last year, our team even acted out scenarios to help friends prepare for multiple mini interviews.

What is our biggest piece of advice? Have fun! This is your chance to shine and tell people what you are passionate about. It is also exciting to hear about your interviewers' experiences working with and teaching students at the school you are interviewing at.

This chapter will give you the inside scoop on how we prepare for interviews and what the interview trail is really like. Enjoy!

If you have additional questions or need help with interviews, feel free to contact The Cracking Med School Admissions *team at* **info@crackingmedadmissions.com.**

PREPARATION

Should I tell my employer about my interviews?

Deciding whether to tell your employers that you are applying to medical school is always a tricky, political situation. Here are some factors to consider: how long you have worked at the company; the firm's expectations of how much longer you will work there; and the effects it may have on getting promoted.

Here are some Pro's and Con's to telling your boss.

Pro's
- Transparency with the organization
- Your boss can write your letter of recommendation
- You can work with your boss and company to schedule the best times for interviews
- Possibility of letting you work remotely even if you are on the interview trail
- Company may grant you unpaid leave to work on applications

Con's
- Your company may not invest as much time and resources into you because it knows that you will be leaving the firm
- May hinder opportunity for promotion
- The organization may not give you as many opportunities (e.g. choosing certain projects or working on exciting side projects)

How do I change or cancel my interview dates?

So you got an interview invitation – CONGRATULATIONS! But the problem is, you can't make the interview dates they gave you as options. So, what should you do?

While interview dates are planned well in advance, it is possible to switch or to choose interview dates. Most medical schools give you a list of options for interview days anyway. Remember, medical schools granted you an interview for a reason – they are interested in admitting you.

The admissions office also consists of human beings who want to help you get into medical school. From our experience, it is definitely do-able to work with admissions offices to get an appropriate interview date nailed down.

HOW DO I SCHEDULE INTERVIEWS IF I AM ABROAD?

If you are abroad, try to cluster your interviews together around the same time frame. Most of our friends usually made two interview trail trips that fell within certain times: early fall (especially applicants for MD/PhD's); December / early January (many applicants come back for the winter holiday season); and late winter. Let's say you get an interview in Boston in December: you should tell all the schools in the Northeast that you will be visiting for interviews.

Here is a sample email you can write to the Admissions office regarding interview date availabilities:

Dear X Admissions Committee:

X School is one of my top choices for medical school because of its strong interdisciplinary programs, support for student initiatives, and location in New York City.

I would like to inform the admissions committee that I will be in the New York area the first week of December.

Thanks,
[Insert name here]

In general, the flexibility of a medical school in granting you interviews depends on how strong of an applicant you are and what school you are applying to. If you get a chance on your application, tell the admissions office that you are abroad. It can only make your life easier!

How do you prepare for interviews?

Rachel: First, I brainstorm my answers to practice interview questions. Second, I do a practice interview once or twice with my friends using the list of questions presented later in this chapter. I usually use different friends so I can receive different types of feedback. Finally, in order to answer, "Why do you want to go to School X," I chat with current medical school students to learn more about what it's like to go to that medical school. For example, I learned that Mount Sinai has take-home exams during the pre-clinical years. This schedule gave the students flexibility with personal obligations. I also learned that my friends at Columbia joined an organization in which they are allowed to be on a transplant team.

James: The best way to prepare for interviews is to know yourself and what you have done well – this may take additional self-reflection on your part. Anything on your application (primary, secondary) is fair game. Therefore, the most basic level of preparation involves knowing your written application backwards and forwards. In open-file interviews, your interviewer will have your entire application available to them to read over before/during the interview. In closed-file interviews, your interviewer will not have had access to your application. In both cases, it behooves you to know your application. In the former case, anything from your application may be asked about - even if you personally may not have thought it was the most salient part of your profile. In the latter case, knowing your application is important so that you can steer the interview to highlight the parts of it that are important to you. If you don't know the interview style of the school, it doesn't hurt to ask the admissions office who might be interviewing you and for how long. Some schools may even provide you with names and biographies of the faculty members that will be interviewing you. In those cases, it can be helpful to get a sense of what the faculty member's interests are. Faculty members do not expect you to know the details of their research, but being aware of what they do is a sign of respect and preparedness that is appreciated in interviewees.

The night before, get a good night's sleep, shower, brush your teeth in the morning, do all the routine things that help present yourself well. If you are staying with a student host, be courteous about the host's schedule and coordinate the day together. Prepare thank-you notes for your interviewers and hosts. These should be considered acts of appreciation, not ways to get an edge on admissions. A lot of time and effort is dedicated to the admissions process!

Rishi: Read as much information as you can on the school's website. You will want to know about the curriculum, student opportunities, mentorship opportunities by faculty members, student groups, research opportunities, leadership opportunities, financial aid, and the culture of being a student. Before each interview, I identified aspects of the school that fit well with my application. During my interview, I worked in examples of opportunities at the school that fit my background.

Talk to current medical students before, during, and after the interview. If you don't have any friends at the medical school you are interviewing at, call the admissions office and ask to be put in touch with current medical students. Talking with medical students will help you understand more about the culture of being a medical student at that school and what students like and dislike about the school.

Be prepared with the logistics of interview day. I like to look at a campus map to familiarize myself with the campus and where I have to be during the day. Make sure you have all the details about your interview and a point of contact at the admissions office in case something happens the day of your interview.

On the day of the interview, I try to learn as much information as I can about my interviewers (especially if their names were not released to me prior to the interview day). It helps to have a smart phone so you can do a quick search or text the names of your interviewers to a friend who can look them up for you during your interview. The point of researching your interviewers is to know more about them so you can create a personal connection.

During an interview, you should be asking the question, "Do I fit in here?" Talk to a lot of students and faculty about what it's really like to study there. I prefer staying with a medical student host so you have the opportunity to have in-depth conversations with current students about the school. When I stayed with a student host, I was able to ask many detailed questions about the school that I was not able to ask during the interview.

THE ACTUAL INTERVIEW

WHAT ARE COMMON INTERVIEW QUESTIONS?

We have compiled some common medical school interview questions and have sorted them out into categories. We hope this will help you prepare!

Common General Questions:

- Tell me about yourself.
- Why medicine?
- What do you see yourself doing in the future?
- Talk to us about your research.
- What have you been doing since graduation?
- Is there anything else I should know about you/tell the admissions committee?
- What will you bring to the med school class?
- When did you know that you wanted to go into medicine?
- Why [Insert medical school here]?

Personal Background & Qualities:

- What did you spend your time doing in high school?
- Tell me about a time when you failed.
- What is your family like?
- What is the hardest thing you have had to deal with?
- What do you like to do in your spare time? What do you like to do for fun?
- What is a typical weekend like for you?
- What do your parents do?
- Where are you from?
- Where were you born?
- What would your friends say is your best quality? What would they say is your weakness?

College / Post Grad:

- Did you like [insert your undergraduate school here]?
- Why did you choose your major?
- What activities were you involved with in college?
- What was your most memorable moment at [insert undergraduate here]?
- Best science/non-science class during your undergrad?
- What would you do differently if you repeated your undergrad?
- What did you write your thesis on?
- What aspect of undergrad did you enjoy most?
- What did you enjoy least or wish you could have changed during your undergraduate years?
- What did you do with your time between college and medical school? Why did you want to spend your time doing this?
- Why did you decide to pursue a Masters degree?

Activities:

- Have there ever been instances when you saw a doctor approach an issue with a patient and you thought you would handle it differently?
- What medical experiences made you decide to go into medicine?
- What did you do during the summers? Why did you decide to choose that summer experience?
- What experiences have you had during your internships that let you know you wanted to be a doctor?
- Tell me about your experiences abroad.
- Do you have clinical experience? What did you gain from it? Insights?

- What experience or activity do you think has prepared you for medical school/medicine the best and how?
- What was your most important leadership position?
- Tell me about a time when you worked on a team.

Medical School Thoughts:

- What do you think will be the hardest thing for you in medical school?
- What are you looking for in a medical school?
- Where else have you applied?
- What do you want to improve about yourself in medical school?
- What are things you look for in a medical school?
- What do you want to know about [insert medical school here]?
- What will be the biggest change in medicine 10 years from now?
- Where do you see yourself in 5/10/15/20 years?
- Do you think you will do research while you are in medical school?
- What kind of practice do you see yourself in?

Randoms:

- Do you have any questions for me?
- How do you handle stress?
- What does being a leader mean to you?
- Tell me about your current job.
- Tell me about a difficult moral dilemma you have dealt with.
- Tell me about a time when you've done something you regretted.

WHAT ARE THE DIFFERENT TYPES OF INTERVIEWS?

THE "GET TO KNOW EACH OTHER" INTERVIEW

These interviews involve you meeting a faculty member or current student one-on-one. They typically last thirty minutes to one hour. Generally, these interviews are not stressful and are focused on your activities.

Do not regurgitate your resume. In order to stand out, WOW your interviewers with stories and what motivates you to go into medicine. Be sure to ask your interviewers about their experiences working or studying at the medical school.

TIP: Interview Preparation

Sometimes you are paired up with a professor who is in your field of study. Be prepared to talk about your field in depth and get grilled on your opinions about related subject areas.

THE "SPEED DATING" INTERVIEW

Multiple Mini Interviews (MMIs) are fairly new in the United States. We think about MMIs as speed dating because you move through 10 different interviewers, and each interview is eight minutes long.

Types of questions: Some of the interviews contain team-based activities in which you complete a task with a co-interviewee partner. Other interviews ask you about your thoughts on bioethics topics and your medically-related experiences. Still, other interviewers will give you a scenario in which you have to role play or describe how you would tackle a situation. We recommend using this academic paper published on multiple-mini interviews as reference:

- *Station #1: Dr. Cheung recommends homeopathic medicines to his patients. There is no scientific evidence or widely accepted theory to suggest that homeopathic medicines work, and Dr. Cheung doesn't believe them to. He recommends homeopathic medicine to people with mild and non-specific symptoms such as fatigue, headaches and muscle aches, because he believes that it will do no harm, but will give them reassurance. Consider the ethical problems that Dr. Cheung's behavior might pose. Discuss these issues with the interviewer.*

- *Station #2: A message that recently appeared on the Web warned readers of the dangers of aspartame (artificial sweetener – NutraSweet, Equal) as a cause of an epidemic of multiple sclerosis (a progressive chronic disease of the nervous system) and systemic lupus (a multisystem auto-immune disease). The biological explanation provided was that, at body temperature, aspartame releases wood alcohol (methanol), which turns into formic acid, which is in the same class of drugs as cyanide and arsenic. Formic acid, they argued, causes metabolic acidosis. Clinically, aspartame poisoning was argued to be a cause of joint pain, numbness, cramps, vertigo, headaches, depression, anxiety, slurred speech and blurred vision. The authors claimed that aspartame remains on the market because the food and drug industries have powerful lobbies in Congress. They quoted Dr. Russell Blaylock, who said, "The ingredients stimulate the neurons of the brain to death, causing brain damage of varying degrees."*
Critique this message, in terms of the strength of the arguments presented and their logical consistency. Your critique might include an indication of the issues that you would like to delve into further before assessing the validity of these claims.

- *Station #3: Your company needs both you and a co-worker (Sara, a colleague from another branch of the company) to attend a critical business meeting in San Diego. You have just arrived to drive Sara to the airport. Sara is in the room.*

- *Station #4: Recently, the Prime Minister of Canada raised the issue of deterrent fees (a small charge, say $10, which* *everyone who initiates a visit to a health professional would have to pay at the first contact) as a way to control health care costs. The assumption is that this will deter people from visiting their doctor for unnecessary reasons. Consider the broad implications of this policy for health and health care costs. For example, do you think the approach will save health care costs? At what expense? Discuss this issue with the interviewer.*

— *Station #5: Why do you want to be a physician? Discuss this question with the interviewer.*

— *Station #6: The Canadian Pediatric Association has recommended that circumcisions 'not be routinely performed.' They base this recommendation on their determination that 'the benefits have not been shown to clearly outweigh the risks and costs.' Doctors have no obligation to refer for, or provide, a circumcision, but many do, even when they are clearly not medically necessary. Ontario Health Insurance Plan (OHIP) no longer pays for unnecessary circumcisions.*

Consider the ethical problems that exist in this case. Discuss these issues with the interviewer.

Scoring: Each interviewer gives you a score, and your overall performance during interview day is based on the average of these scores compared to the other students who interviewed at the same time as you.

THE "GET TO KNOW A LOT OF INTERVIEWEES" INTERVIEW

Some schools have group interviews in which you are put in a room with other applicants and you chat with a few current medical students or faculty members. Our approach to these interviews is to go with the flow of the conversation. Don't be the person who dominates the conversation. However, speak up when appropriate and don't be left silent because of other applicants.

THE "MD/PhD" INTERVIEW

MD/PhD interviews are usually two days long. Most MD/PhD interviews question you about your research. Be prepared to talk about your research in depth and where you think your field will progress in the future. We asked our MD/PhD friends for some insights and advice for MD/PhD interviews.

MD/PhD Interview Tips from Daniel Kim

The panel interviews, where you have many interviewers in one room, were actually somewhat fun. You were able to interact with multiple people, and it almost felt more like a group conversation than an interview. During the PhD interviews, they mostly asked about research. They wanted to know if I understood what I was doing and what my contribution was, so that they could gauge whether what I was saying matched with what I had written. If I would give any tips for interviews, I would say to know your research well, know why you want to do an MD/PhD and articulate it well to them, think about your future career, think about role models you can point to who have done the same, and relax!

You'll find on the interview trail that there are some interviewers that you will click really well with, some you definitely won't click with, and many somewhere in the middle. One of my most memorable interviews was with a professor who just happened to pursue a similar off-beat experience after she graduated to one I did after I graduated. After I graduated, I decided that I wanted to re-explore my cultural heritage in Asia in the context of health disparities and stigma and applied to a fellowship to fund that experience. The professor I talked to just happened to apply to the same fellowship and spent some time working with a marginalized group of individuals in Asia and understanding how that stratified culture functioned. We ended up talking about our unique interests in Asian culture and mythology, which somehow segued into deep scientific research questions. I think this experience showed that if you are yourself and bring up topics that truly interest you, you might occasionally find yourself in an interview situation in which the interviewer unexpectedly has similar interests. Not only does that mitigate stress during an interview, but you may also actually find a role model during your interview process.

Questions that come up a lot during the MD/PhD interview:

1. Tell me about your research followed with questions about your research topic. (Know your research well)
2. What do you see yourself doing in __ years? (Any answer suffices as long as you think it through and it sounds plausible)
3. Why an MD/PhD and not one or the other? (Any answer suffices as long as you have thought it through and are passionate about it)
4. How do you see yourself splitting your time? (Usually somewhere between 70:30 to 90:10

research to science is the traditional answer, but who really knows. Try to think about what fits best with your medical and research interests and see what your physician-scientist role models have done it. Honestly there's no right answer to this so any justifiable answer is good. You can maybe even say you don't know and will base your decisions off how graduate and medical training goes. However, it is good to have a rough idea of what you want to say during the interviews).

5. If you had your own lab, what research would you pursue? (Any answer you have thought through well).

6. Who are your role models? (Find a physician-scientist role model to shadow/talk to if you can).

WHAT DO I WEAR TO THE INTERVIEW?

We all believe that you should dress to impress during your interviews.

TIP: Do we believe in wearing traditional colors?

Nope. In fact, we like wearing non-traditional colors like baby pink or lavender so we don't look like everyone else!

For guys: Wear slacks and a nicely pressed dress shirt. We also recommend wearing a tie. A suit blazer is optional, but interviewees usually wear one in cold weather.

For girls: There is more leeway to what you can wear to an interview. You can wear a suit and skirt or suit and slacks. The top can also range from a nice tank top, blouse, or dress shirt. Jewelry and accessories are a nice touch, but don't go overboard.

TIP: Comfortable Shoes During Interviews

At some schools, you walk around a lot. So invest in very comfortable shoes!

SHOULD I BRING ANYTHING ELSE TO THE INTERVIEW?

It's always good to bring an interview folder with two pens (in case you lose one) and paper. We have had some friends bring a copy of an article published in a prestigious medical journal, a senior thesis, or pictures from their travels.

POST-INTERVIEW

DO YOU HAVE ANY TIPS FOR THANK YOU LETTERS?
- Make your thank you notes specific and personalized
- Send the thank you note within one day's time.
- If you discussed something in your interview that requires a follow-up, be sure to include that information in the thank you letter.

Interview To-Do List:

- ☐ Schedule your interview date and accommodations
- ☐ Research the school you are going to interview at
- ☐ Practice interviewing
- ☐ Be sure to have appropriate interview attire
- ☐ Have questions ready about the school
- ☐ Bring pens, a notebook, and materials that you plan to share with your interviewers
- ☐ Be prepared with interview logistics (have your boarding passes, transportation schedule, and housing information ready)
- ☐ Write thank you letters to your interviewers

If you have additional questions or need help with interviews, feel free to contact The Cracking Med School Admissions *team at **info@crackingmedadmissions.com.***

CHAPTER 6. SELECTING SCHOOLS

An admissions officer once told me that selecting a medical school is like choosing a car. You can buy many types of cars that will get you from point A to point B, but they do so in different ways. Cars have different features and emphasize different strengths. Similarly, all medical schools prepare you to become a physician, but the process of becoming a physician and the opportunities that are available to you are unique to each school. Take time to select the medical school that is right for you. Buckle up because medical school is like a long cross-country ride!

If you have any questions, feel free to contact the Cracking Med School Admissions *team at* **info@crackingmeadmissions.com.**

WHAT FACTORS SHOULD I CONSIDER?

Rachel: I considered three main factors when I was selecting schools:

1. Interdisciplinary opportunities: I was particularly interested in interweaving policy, public health, business, and medicine. I wanted an institution that had a business school and was known for cross-departmental opportunities.

2. Advisory and support: Having a very strong advising and faculty support system was very important to me. Stanford, for instance, had a faculty advisor and a clinical skills advisor. I also found out that they had a study skills advisor and personal tutoring for students who were struggling with academics. Need help with your fitness goals? Stanford medical school students had their own personal trainer too!

3. Campus and location: I liked the campus feeling because I felt like there was a strong sense of community. I also chose medical schools that were located in California or major East Coast cities. Now as a medical school student, I relish going to football games and other school-related activities.

Rishi: There are a few things that I think are important when deciding where to go for medical school (in no particular order):

1. *Pass/fail for the first two years of med school:* I'm so thankful that I don't have to deal with any grading or hierarchy for the first two years. Some schools have high pass/pass/fail, which defeats the point of pass/fail. Medical school is stressful, so why pick a school with grades, competition from classmates, and people not willing to share in learning?

2. *Demographics of the patient population that you will be practicing on:* Consider the type of patients you will be exposed to in the region in which you will attend medical school.

3. *Flexibility in taking your exams and flexibility in scheduling your rotations:* Some schools have flex time where you can take your exam over a few days, when you are ready. Others are stricter. Also, in the clinical years, some schools are better at allowing you to be flexible with your rotation schedule. If you wanted to take a month off and do rotations elsewhere or do anything else, whether or not you have that flexibility is something to consider.

4. *Location.* Pick your school based on where you want to be: Do you want to work on your tan during your lunch breaks in mid-February while you are having lunch outside with friends or go to a school where you wonder when the sun will come out and where you lost your mittens?

5. *Culture of the school:* Do you think you fit with the students and the vibe? You may not have the chance to go to admit weekends / second-look weekends, but from what you observe during your interviews, could you imagine yourself going to school there?

6. *Resources available to students:* Schools will differ in resources and opportunities that are available to students. If you need help with a particular subject,

can you get a tutor? At some medical schools, upperclassmen are paid to tutor pre-clinical students, which is a great resource. If you want to start a club, how much funding is available? If you want to go to a conference, how much will your school pay for travel? Are there funding opportunities for the summer?

7. *What type of medicine does a school value and how that fits with your interests:* Schools value different specialties in medicine, and so will medical students. It can be frustrating to go to a school where your passions are not being fostered through research and mentorship. I am interested in primary care, and I started a chapter of Primary Care Progress at Stanford with other like-minded individuals. Think about potential specialties and what you want to get out of medical school.

8. *Match results:* You should look at the latest match results to see the schools and specialties in which students tend to match. A lot of medical students match where they go for medical school.

9. *Class size:* How big and small do you want your school size to be? I love that my class is small (86 students), and very close.

10. *Financial aid:* What is the average debt burden for each medical student? How generous are the financial aid packages?

James: It is often hard to know which medical school to choose if you have offers from multiple schools. At the end of the day though, medical education is fairly similar from school to school in the United States. Even if you have thoroughly researched each school and it is still difficult to make a decision, this is probably a sign that you have multiple good options. Therefore, don't fret too much about making a "poor" decision. You can't go wrong and you will learn the things you will need to in order to obtain an MD degree.

Personally, I made my decision based on availability of strong interdisciplinary programs, family ties to the area, and resources for students provided by the school. Your decision will also be highly individualized.

ADMIT WEEKEND

Should I go to admit weekend?

If you have the opportunity to go to admit weekend, definitely go!

Should I stay with a host?

Rachel: I always enjoy staying with a current medical school student host. Usually, my host accommodates more than one person, so I become friends with the other visiting students. Staying with a host also gives me an idea about the housing on campus.

What should I do at admit weekend?

Rachel: Have fun! My goal during admit weekend was not to go to all the talks, but rather to go to all the social activities so I can get to know my future classmates. I tried to meet a lot of the admitted students, but I usually found myself spending the majority of my time hanging out with one group of new friends. I found that spending time with a smaller group of people allowed me to forge friendships that last a long time. Even if my new friends and I didn't end up going to the same school, we still kept in touch.

What happens during admit weekend?

Each school has its own schedule and mix of events. Here are some of the activities that occur during admit weekend:

- Welcome speech by deans
- Mini medical school class – see what a discussion class is like
- Attend actual medical school class lectures
- Activities fair
- Hosted dinners
- Academic advisor meetings
- Financial aid: ask questions to the financial aid officer
- Scavenger hunt around the city
- Social activities: bowling, trivia night, bar hopping, clubbing
- Visit community partners / potential extra-curricular activities

---

SELECTING SCHOOLS TO-DO LIST:

☐ Consider the factors that you want in a medical school
☐ Talk to as many students and faculty members as you need in order to feel confident in knowing the range of opportunities available to medical students
☐ Go to admit weekend to learn about the medical school and meet future classmates
☐ If you cannot go to admit weekend, ask the admissions office for students who can answer your questions
☐ Once you decide on a medical school, don't look back!
☐ Do not forget to let your recommenders know which school you decided on

PERSONAL STATEMENTS FROM SUCCESSFULLY ADMITTED APPLICANTS

If you have additional questions or need help with your essays, feel free to contact The Cracking Med School Admissions *team at **info@crackingmedadmissions.com**.*

Name: Sally Baxter

Medical School: University of Pennsylvania

She stared at me with frightened eyes. A nineteen-year-old girl from the rural Chinese countryside, she had traveled several hundred miles to this hospital in Xi'an to have her gallbladder removed. Lying down on the operating table, her eyes had frantically searched the operating room until they fixed on me. Perhaps this was because of all of the strange figures in scrubs that she could see, I was the only female.

"Doctor," she whispered, "will I be okay?"

Holding her hand, I told her in my American-accented Mandarin that everything would be fine. She thanked me and closed her eyes, preparing herself for the operation ahead.

Little did she know that I was not yet a doctor, but like her, just a nineteen-year-old girl in a foreign place. I was an American student intern at this Chinese hospital, getting my first immersive clinical experience. However, my interest in medicine began much earlier. In high school, I fell in love with biology after studying neuroscience and genetics at the California State Summer School for Math and Science. The next year, I worked on a gene therapy project at the Salk Institute and first grasped how the power of science might be harnessed to help those in need by battling disease. In addition to science, I was also passionate about service work, like playing piano for nursing home residents and tutoring children. Medicine seemed to offer the best of both in one tidy package. This prompted me to volunteer at a Sharp Rees-Stealy clinic. Though I enjoyed interacting with the clinic staff, I had very limited patient contact.

Upon arriving at college, I yearned for more interaction with patients. My first year, I started interning at the Duke Brain Tumor Center. I took medical histories and conducted neurological exams on patients. By doing these exams and presenting cases to the physician assistant and the attending physician, I got my first real taste of medicine.

If that was like being fed the first spoonful, then interning in China was like being drenched by an overflowing bucket. The sheer number of people needing care overwhelmed me at first. For instance, I observed doctors who saw close to 100 patients in the span of a few hours during their afternoon clinics. I shadowed physicians and assisted with patient care, but I also engaged everyone around me in conversation. I often talked about life in the U.S., since that intrigued many. But mostly I listened. The patients, students, nurses, physicians – everyone had interesting stories.

I realized that, far from what I naively believed in high school, medicine is not a straightforward combination of science and service. In fact, it is quite messy. I remember a woman in the cardiac intensive care unit crying every day because the cost of her treatment was making her family homeless. Or the resident confessing that because his parents had forced him into this career, he often feared he was giving less than ideal care. There was the joy of a young mother with her newborn, juxtaposed with the sadness of a dying ovarian cancer patient virtually next door.

The intricate stories and interactions touched me. What impressed me most was that even in the most trying situations, the doctors always gave their best. They listened closely and worked carefully, despite grueling hours and high patient volume. Like the doctors I have worked with in the U.S., they dealt with challenges with grace and compassion. In no other profession is there such an intimate human touch and commitment to healing. Instead of being threatened by the messy art of medicine, I was drawn to it even more.

At the same time that I was discovering the humanity of medicine, I was also developing an intense interest in its scientific side. The project that has impacted me the most has been my work in Nina Sherwood's lab at Duke. Dr. Sherwood had engineered flies whose genomes resembled those of human spastic paraplegia patients. In some cases, the flies even expressed human genes! My task was to understand how temperature treatment would affect these mutant flies. I discovered that raising flies in the cold improved their motor function and survival. Before, the flies could not jump nor fly. When crawling, they dragged their hind legs. With my treatment, however, the flies could crawl faster, and a few of them could even jump and fly! Seeing these improvements, even in flies, excited me. Not only could this potentially be applied to improve motor function in paraplegic patients, but it could also shed light on why hypothermia works in other clinical situations, like reducing neurological injury after cardiac arrest and stroke. That is why I am investigating the cellular basis for this effect. While I am unsure of how exactly this would be applied to humans, establishing a first step toward a new therapy is thrilling.

Given my experiences at the bench and at the bedside, I know that medicine is my calling. I also know challenges will arise. However, I hope that with my experiences, a wonderful support network of mentors, and the skills I have gained being a student, researcher, and athlete, I will meet those challenges successfully.

All I hope is that one day, I will be called "Doctor" not by mistake, but because I will have rightfully earned it.

"Maa go, bachao!"

A desperate cry echoed through the hollow corridors of the government hospital. Curiosity led me to investigate, and I encountered an elderly man who had been in a terrible accident. His wounds and pain had not yet been addressed, and all I could do was hold his hands and assure him that he would soon receive medical care. Unfortunately, this was a common occurrence during my time as a volunteer at the Paramount Hospital in my hometown, Serampore, India. There always seemed to be a shortage of doctors and an abundance of patients. Conditions were unhygienic and infrastructure was inadequate. I often had to fight back tears, wishing I could do something more for those in unbearable pain. That was when I pledged to myself that I would become a doctor.

After completing high school, I was confronted with the choice of enrolling in medical school in India or studying in a college elsewhere. Knowing that I wanted to experience and contribute to healthcare at a global level, I decided to pursue a medical career in the United States due to its undeniable impact on global healthcare. Over the past four years, I sought after hands-on medical experiences in both developed and developing communities throughout the world by shadowing physicians in India, Kenya, Canada, and the United States. It was apparent that healthcare facilities between the developing and developed world were poles apart due to the absence of advanced medical technologies in third world nations. In Kenya, I was astounded to see that anesthesia was pumped by hand by an attendant, while patients drifted in and out of consciousness even as doctors were operating on them. Without sophisticated tools and equipment, diagnosis and treatment of diseases can be extremely difficult in the developing world. Furthermore, inadequate funding and limited resources challenge the ability of hospitals to provide treatment to the underprivileged. I spent some time with a boy who had a swollen abdomen in Kenya, but the doctors could not diagnose his condition because his family could not afford the costs of the tests. I recognized the critical need for cost-effective medical technology for the developing world, and this triggered my interest in biomedical research.

In order to learn the fundamentals required for medical research and to become acquainted with novel medical technologies, I majored in Molecular Biology and minored in Biomedical Engineering at Cornell University. My first encounter with scientific research was in the Harvard Medical School Summer Program, where I studied the RIG-I signaling pathway that elicits antiviral immunity. This experience inspired me to work in a molecular medicine laboratory at Cornell University, where I investigated the role of the NF-kB signaling pathway in cellular transformation in breast cancer. Both these experiences allowed me to understand the importance of underlying molecular mechanisms of diseases, which can be a vital part of designing appropriate treatments for patients.

After spending two years studying molecular biology, it was important to me to explore more relevant translational research. Therefore, I opted to work for two years before medical school on the Circulating Tumor Cells (CTC) Project at the Massachusetts General Hospital Cancer Center. The CTC project incorporates a microfluidic device that allows the capture and analysis of circulating tumor cells from the peripheral blood of cancer patients. This promising technology could potentially be used to detect cancer, as well as monitor the progress of the disease and the response to treatments. In developing nations where a biopsy could cost a fortune, a cheap and easy diagnostic test for cancer such as the CTC technology could be used in the early detection of cancer in millions of people. Working on this project has enabled me to contribute to the development of a pioneering technology and has brought me closer to my dream of tackling global healthcare problems through inexpensive medical technology.

Although I come from a small town in India, I have been fortunate to work in a variety of healthcare settings, ranging from rural hospitals in developing countries to cutting edge research laboratories in the United States. It was fascinating to work with a truly diverse group of people, sometimes even without speaking their language. The challenges of traveling and adapting to foreign countries and cultures have taught me to be flexible and resourceful. At the same time, a rigorous academic curriculum and extensive research experiences have instilled me with the confidence to pursue medicine and research. I hope and believe that these attributes, combined with strong determination and unwavering persistency, will enable me to become a physician capable of helping individuals in need. The cries of the elderly man from my hometown hospital and the sight of the Kenyan boy's swollen abdomen remain fresh in my mind, and thus with a strong medical school education and an opportunity to continue research, I aspire to develop and deliver medical technologies to such people.

It was a cold day in Northern Arizona as I prepared for my first attempt at 7 feet in the high jump, a new personal best. My teammates gathered around and began an encouraging clap. The judges gave me the white flag, signaling that they were ready for me to initiate my approach. As I began my run, I could feel the energy from the crowd and my teammates. Everything felt just right as I planted my foot and leaped into the air. My body grazed the bar on my way down but it stayed up. I did it! I jumped over 7 feet!

The high jump epitomizes my life- always jumping over barriers. Whether competing in sports or in the classroom, I have always been able to achieve and excel. I did not begin Track & Field until my sophomore year in high school, but in a short time I worked hard enough to become one of the top high jumpers and long jumpers in the country. More significantly, I overcame personal obstacles, such as a childhood speech impediment and severe shyness. I became my high school Associate Student Body President and successfully delivered a commencement speech to over 3,000 attendees at graduation. Today, I am confident in my abilities to overcome barriers and prove myself on any stage. I am eager to continue growing both personally and professionally on my way to becoming a physician.

Division I intercollegiate athletics, more than anything, has taught me discipline and perseverance. As a high jumper and long jumper for the UCLA Men's Track & Field team, I am constantly challenged to be in top physical and mental shape in order to compete against the best collegiate athletes in the country. Our team workouts are long and intense, and performance expectations are high. Balancing these demands with the challenges of being a student at a highly competitive university, coupled with a demanding undergraduate major, has prepared me well for the rigors of medical school.

Track & Field competition spans the majority of the school year and requires me to maintain a dedicated and strict training regimen. I must also endure a demanding travel schedule that requires me to miss valuable in-class instructions, and take many tests, including final examinations on the road while preparing for competition. This protocol was especially challenging as I transitioned from high school to college.

It took time for me to adjust to the demands of being a collegiate student-athlete, but my current academic achievements are a direct result of reflection, recommitment, and refocused effort as I embraced my calling to become a physician. This maturity demonstrates the balance I have achieved among athletic, academic, and social activities.

Being a student-athlete at UCLA has also provided me with many rewarding opportunities to give back to my community. I have been fortunate to participate in a variety of activities, ranging from mentoring aspiring athletes from the inner city of Los Angeles to playing with and encouraging sick children at the Mattel's Children's Hospital at UCLA. Providing motivation to these children has enhanced my personal growth, made me aware of and compassionate towards others' lives, and has inspired me to be a positive influence on children and underserved communities.

My aspiration to become a doctor became much more apparent after an injury during my sophomore year in college. I landed awkwardly in the long-jump pit during the PAC-10 championships, which resulted in a hyperextended knee and a torn meniscus. My injury required two corrective surgeries, but also allowed me time away from competitive sports to reflect and realize that there was much more to life than athletics. I needed to work much harder on academics to achieve my aspirations and potential to become a doctor. Additionally, my injury allowed me the opportunity to develop a personal relationship with our team physicians, many of whom have become advocates and mentors in my pursuit of entering medical school. I adjusted my focus and recommitted my efforts to become a more dedicated student-athlete, with the goal of becoming a physician.

I have invested hundreds of hours in medicinal settings to better prepare myself for this journey. Through Care Extenders, an internship program at UCLA for students interested in the medical profession, I was afforded rotational assignments in Orthopedics, Critical Care, Radiology, and the Emergency Room. I was also able to network with and shadow doctors at various hospitals and clinics to gain hands-on learning experiences. I have witnessed everything from patients with simple bruises to those with life threatening illnesses, and have been blessed enough to observe a number of surgical procedures as well. Currently, I am working on both human and animal clinical research projects with UCLA physicians in the orthopedic and cardiothoracic specialties. These personally rewarding and enriching experiences have validated to me that medicine is my life's calling.

For me, life is one big track meet. Now, the bar is set at the next barrier: becoming a caring and compassionate physician. I am on the runway and ready to start my approach. My family and friends are in the crowd, providing me with love, encouragement and support. All I need now is for the judges to give me the white flag.

Name: Jonathan Wilen

School: University of Pennsylvania

She threw her head back and reached her venous, textured hand toward the underside of her opposite arm. Knowing she should not interfere, she whipped her hand back across her body. As she repeated this rocking motion, the elderly woman with cheekbones pointing beyond her eyes let out severe moans, prickling the hairs down my spine. In front of me, her son was pacing and running his trembling hand through his thinning hair. He turned to the head ER nurse and spoke as calmly as possible with his mother in such obvious pain, "Is this absolutely necessary?" As a 14 year-old about to enter my first year of high school, I asked myself the same question as I witnessed the frail woman in agony for just a small vial of blood. "If we want to find out what's wrong with her, we need to run a blood test." The ER nurse motioned for me to come closer to the patient. My feet felt cemented to the tiled floor, and I was hoping I did not look as frightened as I felt. I willed myself next to the nurse and patient, "See how small the veins are? It why she's in so much pain."

Eventually we left the elderly woman's room and continued to the other rooms of the ER. I tried to keep a mental map of the health care professionals buzzing around me. Doctors and nurses seemed to create an overwhelming ocean of scrubs, ebbing and flowing from patient rooms, administration desks, and supply rooms. However, as I saw more patients throughout the day, the tempo of the ER seemed to slow to a saunter. The pace of the health care team did not change, rather something within myself allowed for sudden comprehension of the hospital's workings. Asking more questions, I gained an appreciation for the mechanism of the ER. The harmony showed its presence amongst the seeming chaos. With each new patient, my curiosity and fascination grew. As my first day of volunteer training ended, my feet now had trouble staying on the ground.

Ever since that first medical experience, I have tried to discover the change that spawned my initial fear into my current fervor for medicine. Medicine appealed to me at an early stage because I excelled in my science classes and my father is an inspiring physician. After volunteering in the ER, I began to realize that medicine is a career that requires, and moreover offers, much more than excellence in science.

The culmination of my medical and non-medical experiences has strengthened my inspiration to become a physician. Achieving an ambitious and worthy goal requires the commitment of all members of a team. In 2006, my high school hockey team exemplified this notion, winning the Pennsylvania State Championship with a 26-0 record. In medicine, I have witnessed this same teamwork save lives in the ICU of a hospital and in the OR of an obstetrics unit. Being a contributing member of a team with the common goal of saving lives is one of the main reasons I am pursuing a career in medicine.

A health care professional can be defined, at least in part, in the manner they interact with patients. This became evident to me while volunteering in a hospital unit. Interacting with different patients, I found complaints about doctors were never in reference to incompetent medical decisions. Rather, grievances referenced failure in empathy or sensitivity by members of the health care team. Accordingly, patients praised my simple acts of compassion in feeding them a slice of peach or wiping their mouths after eating their lunches. Their compliments led to a sense of self-approval, a motivating emotion I would like to continue to earn throughout my career as a physician. These experiences taught me that medicine involves people, and not just perfunctory treatments of diagnoses.

The characteristics that I see as important in a doctor mirror the personality traits I would like to encompass as an adult - the ability to work seamlessly as part of a team, an unwavering work ethic, respect, compassion and courtesy when interacting with others, and an excitement to learn and improve every day. Thus, by pursuing a career in medicine, I am simultaneously pursuing the path to becoming a better individual of society. In addition to these goals, an underlying fascination of science and physiology foreshadows a rewarding career as a physician. Understanding how things work, and more importantly why they might not work, has allowed for a degree of comfort in some of the more demanding undergraduate pre-medical courses.

Thinking back to that first day of volunteering, I imagine now that I must have caught glimpses of nurses and doctors reviewing patients' charts together, perhaps a coloring book next to a child's bed (a gift from one of the nurses), and the overall teamwork and work ethic of the health care professionals. This all registered at an unconscious level and allowed me to feel more comfortable as that day progressed. It took several years and repeated exposure to these occurrences to acknowledge why I was so drawn to medicine that day and every day since. With the revelation that my strongest traits match my image of an ideal physician, my foundation in a career in medicine has never felt stronger. Having this fundamental, underlining core propelling me to a career in medicine, I am prepared for the excitement and rigors of medical school.

Name: Rachel Rizal

Medical School: Stanford

Is the cervix smooth or bloody? If smooth, apply acetic acid for one minute. Examine the cervix. Do you see white lesions? Do the lesions cover over 75% of the cervix? If yes, refer patient to hospital. If not, treat with cryotherapy.

I recited these steps in my head before I performed a cervical cancer screening on my fourth patient, Nina. As a Fulbright fellow in the Philippines, I attended a week-long Visual Inspection with Acetic acid (VIA) training, which made cervical cancer screenings available to impoverished women in remote locations. Although I was initially apprehensive about going to a rural area, I was eager to broaden my knowledge of healthcare in developing countries.

When I met Nina and other patients, I not only educated them about the cause of cervical cancer, but also taught them how to prevent the disease and gain community support. Health education is my passion. Since college, I have advocated a comprehensive approach towards teaching people how to improve their health. At Princeton, I created Health Matters, an organization that taught low-income minorities pertinent health issues. We hosted interactive workshops that demonstrated healthy lifestyles and cooking classes for families. Doctors also spoke on various health topics. I made an effort to put these lessons into a cultural context so individuals could integrate them easily into their daily lives. At the VIA program and community health centers I volunteered at, I was able to incorporate health education in a clinical setting and extend my experiences in developing nations.

An attending physician watched me as I applied acetic acid to Nina's cervix. Nina winced at the discomfort. A look of nervousness covered her face as she asked, "What if I have cancer?" "Don't worry. Let's do the exam first. Remember the breathing technique we practiced," I said in Filipino as I held her arm and breathed along with her. Nina relaxed and I continued the exam.

I saw it. There was a white layer of lesions around the squamo-columnar junction. I stared in surprise. The thin layer looked more opaque than the dozens of examples I saw on the practice slides. I called the attending and she confirmed the VIA-positive diagnosis. I felt the power of science because I was able to use something as simple as acetic acid to diagnose women who would otherwise have limited access to pap smears.

This was the first time I was given full responsibility of telling a patient she had a disease. I will never forget Nina's face. As tears rolled down her cheeks, I could see apprehension, distress, and shock all at once. I listened intently to Nina's worries – including her two babies and her husband who worked overseas. We devised a plan together on the best way to pursue treatment and discussed how her neighbors and healthcare providers could support her. I gave her confidence by explaining, "This is actually good news. Because we caught the cancer early, it's very treatable." Although nothing could have completely prepared me for dealing with Nina's emotional grief, I found my experience extremely rewarding because I knew that since we caught the cancer early, she would likely beat the disease. Nina left the clinic reassured despite the unexpected news. I felt that it was a privilege to work with Nina and to have her trust me with sensitive health issues. I will continue to use my abilities and future skills from medical school to help more patients like Nina.

I loved many aspects of the VIA training program, and the experience reaffirmed why I want to pursue medicine. I believe I have a gift for teaching others and driving home important concepts to remember. Moreover, I enjoy being with patients throughout the whole process, from discussing the procedure to analyzing their test results. Finally, the advancement of medicine intrigues me. I am amazed with our knowledge of the microscopic HPV and how we used it to develop a vaccine against cervical cancer; it is remarkable that we have invented various methods to detect and treat cervical cancer.

I believe being a doctor is about helping patients and using my clinical experiences to make a greater impact in healthcare. My vision is to integrate medicine, public health, public policy, and business to make medications and affordable healthcare delivery programs accessible globally. I have built a strong foundation in these areas since high school. I have an understanding of the business strategies of medical companies because of my experience at healthcare consulting firms. My senior thesis on vaccine introduction in middle-income countries and internship with the World Health Organization to increase Hepatitis B vaccine coverage in Manila gave me theoretical and practical insights on how international organizations work with governments to increase preventative healthcare. My clinical research on the demographics of Filipino women diagnosed with cervical cancer showed me how clinical practice can influence policymaking. Medical school will provide me with a deeper understanding of how the body is orchestrated and how diseases break it down. Armed with these skills, I will strive to impact the lives of more patients like Nina and increase healthcare access around the world to leave a lasting footprint in medicine.

"Can't you hold her still?" asked the nurse as our patient flailed on the table. I gripped the patient's forearm with one hand and grabbed the surgical tubing tourniquet with the other. Our patient had been brought in for a stab wound to the back, but what should have been a simple blood draw had dragged on for 20 minutes. I could see track marks covering her arms and a stub covered in scabs for her left ear. "It's probably meth," the nurse would tell me later, "Notice how her wounds don't heal." This type of situation is commonplace for the personnel in the shock trauma center of the Baltimore hospital where I volunteer, but not for a midshipman at the U.S. Naval Academy. The nurse uncapped one more needle and on her fourth try she got the requisite tubes of blood.

This is not how I pictured modern medicine. However, I am grateful to see the real challenges of medicine without any idealistic filters. I have always been interested in medicine, but in the past three years I have seen medicine from a much more personal perspective. Volunteering certainly informed my interest, but I was impacted infinitely more by my older sister's losing battle with cancer. Over the course of 17 months from 2005 to 2007, I witnessed her doctors and surgeons race to treat her rare cancer and they inspired me with their efforts to cure her disease. In the end they were not successful, but they showed real compassion and interest in human dignity. The scientific and intellectual satisfaction of diagnosis and treatment appeals to me, but it is the fundamentally human aspect of medicine that makes it my desired vocation.

Over the past few years I have sought out experiences to confirm my interest and deepen my understanding of medicine. While studying on a foreign exchange semester last year in Colombia, I worked with a local volunteer organization providing care to indigent patients in the poorest sections of the city of Cartagena. Having developed some fluency in Spanish, I also volunteered in a free clinic back in Annapolis, often translating for Latino patients who could not speak English. There, I saw physicians deftly assemble necessary facts from patients in spite of frequently complex symptoms and their lack of previous medical care. Working with Naval Medical Research Center (NMRC) last summer allowed me to participate to a small degree in the effort to create a vaccine for malaria. I was fortunate to have the opportunity to work with brilliant military and civilian doctors and scientists developing treatments and vaccines for diseases that are uncommon in our country. Diseases like malaria, Chagas' disease, and dengue fever afflict many impoverished peoples in other countries, but my first exposure to these ailments came during my time at NMRC. Also, it was in research that I observed first-hand how excellent medical leadership can make the difference between success and failure. I will extend this research experience this summer by working at our Navy's tropical disease research unit in Lima and Iquitos, Peru. After seeing the work done by physicians in both clinical and research settings, I can think of no other profession that has the potential to improve lives to the degree that medicine does.

Jonas Salk once said that "Our greatest responsibility is to be good ancestors." For me, that means uniting the interest and talents I possess with the right education to leave this world somewhat better for my having been a part of it. My interest lies in medicine. I know that getting the right education is very important. It will help me to better serve people is situations like my sister's and it will help me be a better ancestor. I hope that the education that I have been so fortunate to receive and the unique experiences I have had will help me to make positive contributions. Yet I know that within medicine, what I contribute will depend on the education I receive and the motivation I provide.

I am very grateful for the education and opportunities I have been afforded and I am eager to devote my life to medicine and serve as a physician. That said, I respectfully request that I be given the opportunity to obtain the education necessary to achieve this goal. I know that with this education I will be able to fight my part of the world's fight and in doing so live up to my greatest responsibility of being a good ancestor.

Name: Victor Alcalde

School: University of Pennsylvania

One of my treasured toys as a child was a flimsy microscope set with poor directions on how to prepare slides of leaves. Growing up I was fascinated by the world around me and my parents encouraged my curiosity and thirst for knowledge. When given a "real" toy, a remote control car from Radio Shack, I frayed the wires, inserted them into an electrical outlet, and marveled at the erupting stream of sparks--also discovering that my parents did not encourage all curiosity equally. It is not surprising that my parents predicted I would become a scientist even before I could spell "hypothesis."

I was only six years old when my father died after a battle with cancer that began before I was born. At that age I did not understand the finality of death, and for weeks after the funeral I continued to think that he might return. After finally accepting that this was impossible, I vowed to grow up to become a doctor, hoping to one day find a cure so that no other kids with sick parents would experience the same loss. That naïve pledge of a six-year-old had a lasting impact by maturing my general interest in science into a fascination with the human body and health.

To support our family, my mother took jobs as a housekeeper while attending courses at a technical school to become a nursing assistant. In my free time, I would flip through her paperback textbooks and pretend to understand what I was reading. Ultimately, my interest in science and medicine was reflected in school, where I exhausted the math and science curriculum of my middle school by the 7th grade and upon graduating high school had taken sixteen AP tests.

As a college student I sought out opportunities to explore clinical and biological research. I was an assistant in an exercise physiology lab during my sophomore summer and then participated in a Harvard Stem Cell Institute internship in Doug

Melton's lab the following summer. The opportunity to contribute to research while learning cellular and developmental biology hands-on invigorated me with a new academic confidence and provided the basis for further research, culminating in my senior honors thesis. Since graduation, I have been working as a lab manager and research assistant at a start-up immunology lab at UCSD. The experience has reaffirmed my desire to include research in my medical career, while also allowing me to develop the tools necessary to excel in that role. Managing a newly established lab and teaching graduate students as they join our group have also underscored my interest in incorporating leading and teaching as additional important roles in my career as a physician-scientist.

While the loss of my father sparked an early interest in medical science, my mother's experiences with healthcare have developed my parallel interest in the social aspect of medicine. It is only recently that my mother has managed to receive medical insurance; she did without it for more than a decade because it was unaffordable for her. When ill, she avoided the doctor and preferred to self-medicate and drink herbal teas. Once, while I was a senior in high school, we were visiting my father's grave when my mother collapsed due to low blood pressure brought on from donating blood a half hour earlier. She slipped in and out of consciousness as my brother and I looked for help. We tried to find a phone in order to call an ambulance but were called off by my mother, who in a moment of consciousness warned us not to because it would be too expensive. We called regardless and the paramedics arrived and stabilized her condition.

As a child, my mother's avoidance of medical care for financial reasons seemed normal. I associated her teas more with her self-reliance and independence than with a barrier set up by high costs. Now, of course, I realize that she would have behaved differently if medical care had been accessible and am saddened that for more than a decade she needed to risk her health to avoid incurring deeper debt. I am further disheartened that even though she is now insured, it is still necessary for her to travel home to our native Colombia for affordable medical care.

Reflecting on these experiences with inequities in our healthcare system has inspired me to volunteer at a student-run free clinic in San Diego as a social resources coordinator and translator. Helping poor patients access a variety of economic and social resources has been gratifying, but I have found translating for Spanish-speaking patients to be the most rewarding. I recently had one patient, a diabetic man, overwhelmed with gratitude at my translating, offer to repair my car at his shop. I did not tell him his offer would be expensive for me--since it required that I first purchase a car--but it helped me realize how much my background and Spanish fluency allowed me to empathize with and better serve this underserved community.

My love of science and personal experiences with the limits of healthcare drives me to a career as a physician-scientist and an advocate for improving access to care. I hope to blend the unique set of experiences that have made me effective at the clinic with my long-held passion for advancing my medical understanding in order to contribute to the continuing improvement of medical care.

"Oh those people just aren't our market," answered a healthcare entrepreneur at the HealthCampDc 2009 conference in response to my question: "What should be done to make online health resources accessible for underserved populations?" In that moment I found myself simultaneously disillusioned with the ideal that healthcare is a right and filled with new resolve to ensure that it is. My career vision crystallized, bringing together my diverse interests in medicine, technology, public health, and education. I seek to practice medicine as an advocate for the underserved and champion of technologies that will revolutionize healthcare.

My diverse interests developed due to a similarly varied personal background. From a young age I have always been interested in medicine. I looked up to my father who is a doctor and research scientist. He taught me how to take one's blood pressure, find one's pulse, and listen to my brother's lungs with a stethoscope. My younger brother was a severe asthmatic which meant frequent visits to the emergency room that further inspired me to one day be able to treat him and other asthma sufferers.

Growing up as an immigrant in multiple cultural settings instilled in me a greater appreciation for cultural sensitivity in healthcare. My parents emigrated from China to study in Europe. Consequently, I was born in Switzerland, spent my childhood in England, and then moved to the San Francisco Bay Area when I was eleven. Being able to speak Mandarin and Cantonese and understanding the cultural differences between the many Asian ethnicities has eased communication with patients in my volunteering at the Asian Liver Center. When I register patients or assist the nurse in giving vaccinations, patients are always pleasantly surprised when I speak to them in their native tongue. Afterwards, I follow up with educational information on Hepatitis B and make sure patients know when to come back for their next shot. Being able to understand each patient's unique background has made me realize the value of approaching medicine with a broad perspective.

As such, I have explored medicine from a wide range of perspectives, from the macroscopic to the microscopic. My most formative experience was working at the Office of Disease Prevention and Health Promotion while I was in the Stanford in Washington program in early 2009. I was immersed in the world of health policy and population medicine as I helped to lay the foundation for the Healthy People 2020 policy document. Working and studying in D.C. alerted me to the critical needs of health information technology and healthcare reform. This overarching view has given new meaning to my research and volunteering experiences as I was able to see how basic research and non-profit groups can influence policy. While in D.C., I also joined the National Health IT Collaborative for the Underserved, which reinforced my interest in applying technology to end health disparities and help vulnerable populations. With these experiences, I have learned that medicine integrates many fields and thus this has supported my study of computer science as a complement to medicine.

I am majoring in computer science because I want to embrace the potential that technology has in helping and educating people. The ability to program computers has enabled me to make contributions quickly. As the lead developer of Stanford Online, I played an integral part in developing and releasing the free course initiative Stanford Engineering Everywhere (http://see.stanford.edu). During the summer and fall of 2008, I dedicated more than twenty hours per week to ensure that the site launched smoothly. Through our team's work, half a million visitors around the world have benefited from these courses. This work has informed my views on electronic education and how online resources are changing education and healthcare for patients. As a result, I will be uniquely poised to approach the rapidly growing fields of electronic health and health information technology.

Each new discipline I learn provides a unique way of thinking about problems. Studying medicine will offer a perspective and skill set which will not only allow me to serve patients directly but to also be a stronger advocate for patients. My interests have culminated in the honors research I am currently conducting on barriers to adoption of personal health records (PHRs) in the underserved. I am working directly with patients at Mayview, a safety-net clinic serving Santa Clara County, California, to see how PHRs may most effectively be adopted and used. This project serves as a prelude to the bridging of medicine and technology that I will continue to build upon.

I would like to play a role in the translation of new technologies to the clinic in order to improve the practice of medicine. With my background, I will be able to see the big picture, advocate for a solution to make certain that healthcare is a right, implement the solution, and most importantly, see to it that all individuals benefit from this right. The best way to fulfill this role is through the study of medicine.

Name: Peter Roberts

Medical School: University of California,
Davis

As far back as I can remember I have felt connected and intrigued by nature and healing. Chasing frogs in the damp summer air and swaying in pine trees typify my childhood adventures in Florida's lush ecosystem. As a child eager to interact with the outdoors, I filled my backyard with homemade tree forts, swings and contraptions. When a friend of mine fell from the zip-line I had constructed and broke her femur, I felt the inkling of my call to healing.

Despite my love of nature and caring qualities, these inclinations dissipated amongst the commotion of five siblings and weary parents. In a family of seven far below the poverty line, university education was not discussed. The only academic dialogue I can remember came from my mother who would gently ask me, "Did you try your best," while holding my report card. Those seemingly simple words have motivated me throughout my life.

Two weeks after high school graduation I moved 3000 miles to California. Having examined my options, I decided to pursue my interest in health and philosophy via yoga. I enrolled in the Yoga, Service and Community course at Mount Madonna Center. In addition to inspiring an interest in integrative medicine, this choice has formed the bedrock of my discipline and personal growth. I practiced meditation, breathing and stretching early in the morning and studied philosophy books late into the night. I found a joy in living and working with over 80 residents during this seven-year period.

Living a modest life in a cabin deep within those mountainous redwood forests I relished my proximity to nature. Yet this picturesque setting was also home for an inner battle to find my place in the world and the will to attain it. In these years, feeling vulnerable and alone without financial or personal support, I found empathy for those in need and an awareness of the myriad less fortunate than I. Having been diagnosed with ADD I had resigned myself to endure my affliction, yet with the aid of community and healthy living, I grew socially and academically. These experiences of hardship remain at the core of my pull to medicine and my aspiration to help others.

My desire to serve life as a doctor also stems from my fascination with nature, the human body, and the balance that is health. Engaging this, I chose my first ever college and biology course--Anatomy. The scientific intricacies of the human body far exceeded my imagination and I was immediately captivated by its complexity and artistry. "I would love to be a doctor," I said to myself for the first time as I explored the musculature of a gracious donor. I longed to immerse myself in further study.

To fund my education I tried my hand at many careers including sculpting, carpentry, masonry, hotel management, yoga teaching, human resource management, business administration, and research analysis. Always, "trying my best" earned me promotions and recognition in every category. But my heart and imagination remained gripped by the wonder of science, the human body and the call to service. Alongside a dense work schedule, I found time to explore numerous health conferences, talk with health practitioners, or just enjoy science videos.

I further tested these medical and service oriented interests during five years as a firefighter. As a first responder, the majority of calls were medical in nature. In situations ranging from car accidents to cardiac arrests, I savored the fulfillment inherent to helping those in medical crisis and assisting in balancing chaotic scenes. Yet I eagerly wanted to graduate beyond controlling bleeding or stabilizing airways. I desired to assist a full recovery to those trauma patients.

In my current work I experience a satisfying blend of my interests in science, health, and service. Initially I shadowed and assisted with research testing the efficacy of a project offering free integrative medicine to the underprivileged. Now, as coordinator of the project, I have progressed to overseeing all aspects including patient communication, fund raising and community outreach. Serving an area burdened with health inequities, my heart is regularly humbled by the gratitude in patients' eyes for access to our healing services.

This past year at the clinic has been sobering. Inundated with towering paperwork and taxing patient care time limits, my mentor navigates modern medicine. Yet I see his deep fulfillment in providing long-term care to patients and their children. I watch my mentor's eyes light up when they deliver cards with words of appreciation and photos of their healthy family. He helps those who are truly in need and it is inspirational. I have found the experience so meaningful that I would like to follow in my mentor's footsteps and practice family medicine to underserved communities.

Looking back, my life seems like an effort to rediscover and embrace my childhood inspiration, intelligence and hope. Yet this struggle has also emboldened my resolve. Against the background of my life experience I cannot think of any other profession that would utilize my skills or capture my passions as fully as this calling--as a life-long student and teacher in the dynamic, rewarding and challenging profession of health, medicine, and service--as a physician.

Name: Nina Zhao

Medical School: University of Pennsylvania

All I saw was white. It was everywhere – the walls, the sheets, the pillows. Even the curtains were white. I know my grandfather hated it. His favorite color was green, like the color of the gardens he used to stroll through before he was diagnosed with prostate cancer. Now, five years later, the only greenery he could enjoy was the small sprig of bamboo my uncle had placed next to his bed. I had been routinely visiting him ever since my mother and I arrived in China three weeks before. Some days would be good. My grandfather would ask me about my life in the United States, and I would tell him stories. When he laughed, I could see remnants of the person he used to be: the strong soldier who served his country, the playful man who tossed me over his shoulder when I was little. But other days were not so good. On those days, my mother and I would sit at his bedside as he slept fitfully, deep coughs wracking his frail body. Although my grandfather never lost his will to live, the disease ravaged his body, stealing his freedom, his strength, and finally, his personality. The absence of health can bring great suffering, and ultimately, it is my desire to promote health and preserve life that motivates me to pursue a career in medicine.

I took this motivation with me to college and sought out an opportunity to shadow physicians in the Emergency Department at Barnes-Jewish Hospital. As I helped an orthopedic surgeon set a lower leg fracture, I was enthralled by the healing power of medicine. I also found myself particularly drawn towards the moments of teaching that were simultaneously occurring all around me: a resident explaining a course of treatment to a patient, an attending physician guiding an intern through an ultrasound. Here, I saw medicine not just as a way of healing, but also a form of education. I was engaged by this environment of continuous learning and collaboration, and I was excited to have the opportunity to be mentored and to one day become a mentor too.

Advances in medicine and health care cannot be made without innovations in research, and I had the privilege of conducting my own research project in a neuro-oncology lab my junior year. The lab's main objective is to unravel the biology of brain tumors to improve treatments for patients with neurofibromatosis. In particular, my project investigated the role of microglia in the formation of optic gliomas. I swiftly developed my scientific abilities, learning how to design experiments, analyze outcomes, and determine new directions, all while keeping a larger goal in mind. But the most striking lesson I learned was not at the lab bench. The lab's principal investigator is both an accomplished researcher and a gifted clinician, and he would sometimes bring patients to our lab meetings. In one such meeting, the patient was a young girl, no more than eight years old. She sat slightly hunched in her chair, her posture a remnant of the tumor that had both weakened her motor skills and left her with an impaired sense of hearing. Yet neither her youth nor her disabilities prevented her from engaging in the meeting. As we presented our projects, the neuro-oncologist simplified the important concepts and created analogies that she would understand. I found myself deeply moved by the depth of their relationship and the way he was able to help her become an active part of her own care. In this moment, I realized that medicine is about so much more than treatments and procedures; it is also about building the trust that allows one person to truly impact another. As a clinician, I hope not only to provide the same comfort and care to my patients, but also to empower them through knowledge of their own bodies and illnesses.

Ultimately, it was not until I studied abroad in London that I began to understand medicine from an even broader perspective. Over four thousand miles away from home, I studied medical sociology and anthropology and investigated health care systems in an international comparative context. I was immersed in a new culture of health care. In the Minor

Injuries Unit at Guy's Hospital, I saw patients walk in to get a few stitches or to simply have the dressing changed on a wound and walk out in a matter of minutes. But in the general practitioner's office, I learned that while patients were given to him based on location, rather than insurance company, there were also long waitlists even to make an appointment. As I learned how medicine operated in a wider social and political arena, I began to appreciate how the very structure of the health care system can affect patients' lives, and I am eager to explore this concept further in the course of my career.

Regardless of the country, culture, or type of practice, medicine is grounded in the fundamental qualities of compassion and a love for humanity. The long hours I spent in the stark white hospital room with my grandfather taught me empathy and patience. My experiences since then have shaped my interest in medicine from a desire to care for another's wellbeing into an understanding of health care from a more holistic, socially aware perspective. I look forward to merging these lessons with my motivation and intellectual curiosity as I take the first steps forward in my medical education.

Name: Rishi Mediratta

Medical School: Stanford

As I waited in the airport for my flight home to Michigan during my Thanksgiving break freshman year, my Johns Hopkins sweatshirt attracted the attention of a man who was waiting near me, Dr. Richard Hodes. Upon learning that I intended to study public health, Dr. Hodes responded, "Oh, I do that. Come with me. I have some pictures to show you!" He shared with me snapshots of his life and work in Ethiopia, where he has treated patients and taken in over twenty orphaned children for the past two decades. I wrote his e-mail address on a napkin, and we have since corresponded regularly about health issues in Ethiopia.

This correspondence has been the most important factor in motivating my decision to pursue a medical career. The very next semester, Dr. Hodes' work inspired me to write a proposal to conduct a hygiene survey in Ethiopia, for which I secured the Woodrow Wilson Research Fellowship to implement. I made my first trip to Ethiopia during winter break of my sophomore year where I lived with the Hodes family and became acquainted with individuals and communities in a country that was wholly new to me.

I volunteered at Mother Teresa's Mission, a care center that provides a safety net for destitute Ethiopians, most of whom are homeless, orphaned, or terminally ill. I helped the medical staff bathe, feed, dress, and groom patients. One day, Dr. Hodes explained that he needed to leave for an hour to retrieve the syringe and tubes needed to draw a patient's blood. He hoped that I would sit with the young boy in the meantime. Redeye, Dr. Hodes explained, was suffering from MALT Lymphoma, a painful condition characterized by the abnormal growth of cancerous immune cells in the GI tract.

I comforted Redeye as he cried in pain and clutched his stomach. Then he motioned to the pan under his bed, and I handed it to him. I turned my head to give him the privacy he deserved as he urinated into the pan. He was clearly emaciated, and I gently laid my hand on his stomach to keep him warm. Dr. Hodes eventually returned with the tubes. A tourniquet was not available, so I firmly placed my hands around Redeye's upper arm--a makeshift tourniquet--so that Dr. Hodes could find the veins.

At the end of the day, I walked home feeling helpless and overwhelmed. I was a student in one of the best public health programs in the world, pursuing studies in order to understand health and health care inequalities from a broad perspective. Yet all I could do for this suffering young boy was retrieve a bedpan and offer him a warm touch? Not only did I want to do more, I wanted to know more. How did Redeye present with this disease? What needed to be done to improve his condition? How could this disease be prevented in other children?

During the two summers that followed, I immersed myself in child health research, volunteer work, and public health practice in a number of underserved Ethiopian communities. I revised my hygiene proposal specifically to research the risk factors and management of childhood diarrheal disease. During my time in Ethiopia, I had witnessed children unnecessarily dying from this preventable illness and felt I could begin to tackle the disease using my knowledge and resources. My research resulted in the implementation of a health education intervention program to teach mothers to recognize the signs and symptoms of diarrhea and to increase fluid intake during episodes. Even once the program was in place, however, my frustration at the harsh reality of health care in Ethiopia sometimes still overwhelmed me. Why teach mothers how to recognize diarrhea in their children, if there is no health care provider in the clinic when they arrive? Why encourage women to wait in line for days to see a doctor, if the doctor will not have the supplies to help the patient?

The time I spent volunteering in Ethiopia taught me valuable skills that I can use as a doctor. I learned to work under pressure and in teams, as I had to manage 13 health workers to

111

conduct the diarrhea disease research projects. I also learned that although modern medicine can accomplish a great deal, doctors are not always miracle workers and sometimes must face disappointment and sadness. I now understand that education and prevention programs, while important, are only half of the battle in improving the health of individual and communities. I have stayed in touch with Redeye. His face is fuller now and his skin is a healthier tone. But Redeye was one of the lucky ones; not only did he know to seek care, but he also had access to necessary health care resources. Like Dr. Hodes, I hope to devote my career to providing both education and access to care, by training as both a physician and a public health scientist.

Name: Andrew J. Park

Medical School: University of California,

San Diego

"Your Spanish is good, and I think you can handle it. Tell me how it goes." Dr. Witt gave me an encouraging tap on the shoulder with his paperwork as he closed the ER drape.

The patient started to cry, and I did not know what to say.

"Um," I said.

Maria was a young woman of 27 who had just been informed that the bleeding she had endured for the past five days was the result of a spontaneous miscarriage. Her symptoms had initially raised Dr. Witt's suspicions, but a bedside ultrasound confirmed his diagnosis. I strained my eyes on the grainy screen as he pressed the cursor over her belly in disquieting silence. No sign of a fetus. However, while the diagnosis came easily, the disclosure would be difficult: Maria only spoke Spanish. Dr. Witt gave her his impression and left the explanation to me.

Working the graveyard shift as an ER scribe has been a rewarding and inspiring chapter in my pursuit of medicine. Over the course of nine months, Dr. Witt challenged me to take every opportunity to glean knowledge and start thinking like a resident. Under his mentorship, I applied years of collegiate science and research to navigate vitals, analyze lab results, and interpret EKG tracings, and found I thoroughly relished the thrills of medical sleuthing. But Dr. Witt's guidance was more than just intellectual. I watched closely as he interacted with his patients. How he would make room to sit at the edge of their bed, doodling diagrams of valves and vessels on the sheets to better explain their diagnoses. Through his simple Spanish and deadpan demeanor, he would break down clinical findings into layman's terms to ensure that they understood the effect on their lives beyond the thin slice of their ER visit. "Pay attention to their history," he would say. "It's why they – and we – are here."

As a history major, I knew the importance of perspective – the irrefutable value of each person's narrative. History was an intellectual exercise in empathy, a discipline that trained me to analyze facts far removed from my own daily life and experiences. Just as multiple factors influenced people's perception of events, so, too, do cultural, linguistic, and social facets underlie a patient's history and illness.

I saw firsthand the weight of cultural perceptions on health and healing during my summer in Galmi, Niger. My research in the hospital's HIV/AIDS clinic challenged me to discern the effects of cultural stigma on healthcare delivery. Data collected from the neighboring villages showed that local misunderstanding of HIV prevented patients from seeking proper medical care. I remember meeting Sutila, a woman ostracized by her husband and community for having AIDS. She repeatedly declined medications because, ashamed of disgracing her family, she felt she deserved to die. Initially, amidst stories like Sutila's, I felt that there was little I could say in response, besides a simple "Yu Hak'uri (You have my sorrow)." Over the summer, however, I realized I didn't have to say anything at all: by creating theatrical skits that emphasized body language to highlight HIV's misconceptions, I was able to increase local awareness and soften these cultural constraints.

From educating people in Niger to working alongside doctors as a scribe, I have learned the significance of language barriers, not just in the traditional sense between English and Spanish, but also in the medical setting between the healthcare professional and the average person. I find myself stuck in the middle, fluent in neither, but determined to bridge that gap.

For among the many aspects I love about medicine, I cherish most the "translation," enabling each patient to make sense of their individual experience; moving beyond the complex treatment modalities, the conflicting survival statistics, the pain, and arriving at what it means for them. This is what will sustain me through the difficult moments, knowing full well that, what is to me another day at work is very much a vulnerable and oftentimes defining moment of their lives. Medicine, I have come to realize, is itself a language of empathy and thought. It is a language that presupposes the context of each patient's experience: that each patient has a history, not just medical in nature, but a reflection of their individual lives and facets. Medicine is the language in which I want to be fluent in order to connect with others, beyond linguistic or cultural divides.

That night, I found the words I wanted to say. As Dr. Witt left to place orders, I delicately went over Maria's diagnosis in my not-so-fluent Spanish. She listened patiently as I cautiously conjugated each verb to disclose her results. I shared in her disappointments as she set aside her hopes of starting a family. With her story realized, I expressed my sentiments. How it wasn't her fault. How miscarriages happen; her body's way of protecting herself from potential harm. As I spoke, I found my sentences more emotional, less clinical, realizing that Maria needed less medical care, more human comfort. There was still hope for a family. She would be okay. As I finished, she smiled and expressed her thanks. "You'd make a good doctor," she added.

One day.

Name: AML, MD, PhD

Medical School: University of Pennsylvania

They tried to talk me out of it. Or so it seems when I recall early memories that with time have blended together into a collage of moments: gazing up at a periodic table on the wall of my room, my father teaching me about carbonic anhydrase inhibitors and the names of muscle groups before I could read-- juxtaposed with echoing grumbles from two physician parents, "You don't want to be a doctor...Medicine is not what it used to be."

My parents instilled in me a love of questions that in high school developed into a love of forensics and science as tools to find the answers I sought. Debate and mock-trial provided the sound, level foundations of logic and argumentation on which I would place science as a lens through which to view and investigate the macroscopic world. Unlike most medical school applicants, who seem to have known their entire lives that they were destined for medicine, I have known since my freshman year in high school that my interests lay in the biological sciences--biology and not medicine, perhaps, because each was at the time loaded with connotations of a very personal nature. Science, after all, was a quest for qualitative and mathematical answers to the questions of the universe, and at that point in my life, medicine was by no means a part of the equation.

In essence, I held no romanticized illusions about a life in medicine and, though the questions I began to ask frequently gravitated towards topics with implications for the betterment of human existence, I never categorized my curiosity as an interest in medicine--I was interested in biology, and, in my mind, good biology remained closely associated with an interest in the repercussions of research on life.

In college, organic chemistry, genetics, and molecular cell biology quickly won my heart and became the scaffolding, though now on the level of nanometers, on which I built my understanding of biological life-processes. The logical process of investigating a particular protein-protein interaction and the critical thinking required to punch holes in the alternative interpretations of the data, for example, appealed to the mathematician and the logician in me. In fact, the enduring allure of molecular cell biology lay in the overwhelmingly complex, yet elegantly efficient, web of protein and DNA-level interactions that gives rise to organism-level response. But with my attention fixed on phenomena at such a small scale, I often found my attention diverted from the end to the means--from the reason for asking these biological questions to the mechanism for answering them.

I chose to live in the ------------- University Medical School dormitory during the summer of 2002 to facilitate my genetics research under a Howard Hughes Medical Institute fellowship. The unavailability of kosher food at the medical school cafeteria led me to seek dining facilities elsewhere. The hospital cafeteria, located a few heartbeats away from the children's hospital, the ICU, and the emergency room, remained the only location serving food I could eat. Mornings, evenings, and nights, weekdays and weekends, preoccupied with molecular markers and linkage mapping data, I hung my lab-coat on the wall and came to sit and to eat, a healthy adult among the ill and suffering. One particular late night comes to mind, however, when the air-conditioning inside the medical center was particularly zealous, and I left the lab still wearing my lab-coat to hold my body heat. I ordered a turkey sandwich and protein smoothie at the hospital, as was my habit, but as I walked through the cafeteria I noticed something so subtle that on any other day I may not have noticed: a young boy with a walking cast, an old woman hobbling slowly alongside her IV drip, and a middle-aged man in a wheelchair between bouts of wheezing--each smiling at me warmly. I paid for the meal and chose a seat, somewhat unsettled until I glanced at my shoulder and read the boldly embroidered "Department of Genetics." The lab-coat covering my shivering shoulders represented the immense trust these patients had bestowed upon me. Judaism tells of a heavenly court where, after his death, each man and woman must account for every moment spent on earth. I envisioned myself in a court of these peers--each of whom modern medicine had touched in a profoundly tangible way--frantically attempting to justify to them the time I had spent in class and in lab, and the hope they placed in me. The notion that in losing sight of the end goal—an impact on human life--I had betrayed that intrinsic trust overwhelmed me. The distinction between the bench-top and the clinic vanished, and I returned to my lab with a new understanding of purpose.

Neither can I pursue basic science without pondering the biomedical implications, nor can I imagine practicing medicine without a sense of wonder at the interplay of molecule-level processes that causes a patient to present with symptoms, for the synthesis of research and medicine is the religion of hope. Thus I seek the basic science to understand the clinical and the clinical to understand the basic science--two parts of a necessarily integrated whole. Indeed, medicine is not what it used to be, yet it holds the potential to be so much more.

SECONDARY ESSAYS FROM SUCCESSFULLY ADMITTED APPLICANTS

Once you start churning out those secondary essays, you will realize that some of the prompts are asking the same types of questions. In this section, we've given you some sample secondary essays and organized them in different types of questions. If the author wrote essays in one category, we also clumped these essays together so you could see how each author crafted his or her experiences.

If you have additional questions or need help with your essays, feel free to contact **The Cracking Med School Admissions** *team at* **info@crackingmedadmissions.com.**

WHY X SCHOOL?

Many schools are interested in why you want to go to their medical school. Is it the culture that attracts you? Specific professors? The location? As we stated in earlier chapters, don't be generic. Really look into the school's programs and cultures to see what makes them unique and a right fit for you.

Name: Mike Baxter

Why are you interested in attending the University of Virginia School of Medicine?

In my experience with a few alumni of the University of Virginia's School of Medicine, I have been impressed by their combination of superb technical skill with sincere compassion and interest in the patient. I can recall one Virginia graduate consistently treating his patients with dignity, no matter how abrasive or uncooperative. I was impressed by his consistent professionalism and had to admit to myself that it would have been difficult for me to act the same way. The more I looked into his medical school, the more apparent it became that his compassion was a trait of many graduates. The more I learn about UVA's MD program, both in terms of its academic rigor and humanistic awareness, the more I believe it stands to offer me.

Jonas Salk once said that "Our greatest responsibility is to be good ancestors." For me, that means uniting the interest and talents I possess with the right education to leave this world somewhat better for my having been a part of it. My interest lies in medicine. I believe that UVA's School of Medicine has the proven record of success in thoroughly educating physicians and that it can give me the tools I need to turn my interest in medicine into a career. An education from UVA will help me to better serve people in need and to ultimately be a better ancestor. Yet I know that within medicine, what I contribute will depend both on the education I receive and the effort I provide.

I am very grateful for the education and opportunities I have been afforded and I am eager to devote my life to medicine and serve as a physician. I would like to be given the opportunity to attend the University of Virginia's School of Medicine to achieve this goal. I know that with this education I will be able to fight my part of the world's fight and in doing so live up to my greatest responsibility of being a good ancestor.

Name: Jonathan Wilen

*Please explain your reasons for applying to
the Perelman School of Medicine.*

The support of my family is a principal contributor to my success and candidacy for medical school. To continue to succeed in medical school, proximity to my family must be a paramount consideration. My older brother Daniel is currently in his first year of medical school at the Philadelphia College of Osteopathic Medicine. To have the opportunity to practice the art of medicine in the same city as my older brother is simply irresistible. In addition to my familial connections to Philadelphia, I am enthralled by the opportunities at PSM. I am searching for an institution that embraces my philosophy of medicine. By predicating its beliefs of medical education on a commitment to preparing for the health care challenges of the future, PSM is an institution entirely in concert with my goals for medical practice. Operating through world-renowned hospitals and leading facilities in biomedical research, PSM gives me the best opportunity for success in the medical profession.

Name: Rachel Rizal

How will the Stanford curriculum, and specifically the requirement for a scholarly concentration, help your personal career goals?

Stanford's curriculum is ideal because it complements my hands-on learning style and incorporates medicine in a social context. In particular, the Community Health Foundation with an International Application builds on my past experiences. While volunteering in Philippine public clinics, I gained perspective on how to improve service delivery at a community level. With Stanford's strong advising, I will continue to promote health awareness and clinical treatment programs in under-served areas. The school's numerous community partnerships, like Arbor Free Clinic, are powerful learning and research tools.

Stanford is a perfect fit because I can conduct research across departments, such as the Graduate School of Business and Health Research & Policy. The flexible curriculum allows me to pursue electives abroad, joint degrees, and a Traveling Scholarship for long-term projects. The support for student initiatives enables me to share my experiences and future networks with others.

Name: Sally Baxter

What is it about the Cleveland Clinic
curriculum that you feel makes it a good
match for your learning style?

First, the small class size facilitates greater faculty-student and student-student interactions. I learn much better in a classroom of 20 than in a hall of 200, so this is a big plus. Moreover, the PBL seminars provide opportunities for self-directed and discussion-based interactions. I like this active learning style more than passively listening to lectures.

The vast research and clinical opportunities are also huge draws. The rigorous research training and superb mentoring fulfill my desire to further develop my investigational skills. Doing both basic and clinical research is a great way to learn how science translates to medicine. The early clinical exposure also sets CCLCM apart and appeals to my preference of longitudinal learning.

*If you were working on a small group project
and another student didn't carry their load,
how would you handle it?*

Prompt and articulate communication is key. Silence prolongs the problem, causing greater group conflict in the long run. I would approach the person and express the problem in a non-threatening way. For example: "I've noticed that you haven't been coming to our group meetings recently. Is everything okay? We really need your help." When people realize their inaction has been noticed, they usually start working more. Alternatively, there could be a legitimate reason for the slacking. Our group could help the person resolve the issue together. For example, if he/she is having trouble keeping up with other classes, we could suggest time management strategies or study tips. If the situation is more personal, like a death in the family or a broken relationship, I would provide some support and also refer the person to campus counseling services. Whether it takes a gentle reminder or some help with a real challenge, hopefully the person will begin to pull his/her weight in the project.

*Please give your reasons for your interest in
this research Program. Include areas of
research interests.*

My research addiction started in summer 2004. As an intern in Fred Gage's lab at the Salk Institute, I cloned gene therapy constructs for amyotrophic lateral sclerosis (ALS) into various vectors, which were then injected into ALS mouse models. To measure the effects of the therapy, I dragged each mouse's limbs across a metal grid to assess grip strength. The moment of truth came at the end after analyzing the data. Lo and behold, the treated mice had greater strength and motor function than the untreated mice. The same might hold true for humans! It was an "aha!" that showed me just how important research is to medicine.

That was 11th grade. I knew lab techniques, but I did not fully understand underlying principles or experimental design. But the research bug had bitten me, so I probed these deeper aspects in college. My honors thesis project in Nina Sherwood's lab has taken me through the entire scientific process, shaping me into an independent thinker. Other summer research projects have broadened my knowledge and diversified my skill set. Now, I have developed a greater understanding of biomedical research and a deeper appreciation for its potential applications.

I have also seen firsthand the synergistic interaction of research investigation and clinical medicine by working in academic medical environments. At the Duke Brain Tumor Center, I see physicians combining compassionate care with cutting-edge cancer biology and medical imaging research to treat individual patients and advance medicine at the same time. Similarly, I witnessed the potential of bridging research and clinical work while assisting with macular degeneration research at the UCSD Shiley Eye Center.

My career goal is to help move medicine forward via research, thereby making a contribution that could help more people than I could treat directly. To achieve this goal, I will need a solid foundation in science, rigorous research and clinical experience, and helpful mentors. HST provides all of this and more.

With my background in biology and physics, I am prepared for the rigorous and quantitative curriculum. Given my interest in an academic career, I am attracted to HST's research emphasis and unparalleled resources and opportunities as a result of the collaboration between Harvard, MIT, and the Boston teaching hospitals. Its thesis requirement, option of extending program length, and student funding opportunities are clear signs of a commitment to student research.

Currently, I am most interested in research in functional and regenerative medicine, which holds great promise and could potentially be applied to a wide range of clinical situations. My interest in this area is driven by stem cell research experiences at the Salk Institute and at UC-Berkeley. I have also written term papers on the ethics of therapeutic cloning and the application of neural stem cells to the treatment of spinal cord injury, which have been published in Duke's undergraduate journals. I would like to continue learning more in this area and gain hands-on experience in therapeutic technologies and tissue engineering. Faculty members whose work looks particularly interesting are Jeffrey Karp, Shiladitya Sengupta, Ali Khademhosseini, and Utkan Demirci.

The faculty, like the rest of HST, is top-notch. The caliber of the student body is also extremely high, especially given the prominence of Harvard and MIT on the global stage. Combined with the unique possibility of having HST PhD students in MD classes, there would be no shortage of opportunities to learn from my peers. Furthermore, the experience would be enhanced by small class sizes, allowing for more faculty-student and student-student interactions.

HST is an exciting program that fits ideally with my undergraduate background, research interest, and overall career goals. Perhaps if I am lucky enough, it will fuel my addiction for the next four (or more!) years and provide a foundation for lifelong learning and service.

Name: Sally Baxter

Please write a brief statement giving your reasons for applying to Weill Cornell Medical College. Please limit your statement to less than 200 words.

Biomedical research is my passion. Whether it is investigating the genetics of spastic paraplegia, stem cell development, the effects of stress on myelination, or the psychosocial effects of vision loss, I delight in the process of asking questions and expanding knowledge. As someone aspiring toward academic medicine, nothing beats the combination of Weill Cornell's superb clinical training, especially at New York-Presbyterian Hospital, and well-deserved reputation as a research powerhouse. Weill Cornell's collaborations with nearby institutions also offer an unparalleled array of opportunities. Given my experiences at the Duke Brain Tumor Center and my extensive neuroscience research background, I am particularly interested in working at Memorial Sloan-Kettering, the world's foremost cancer center, and in Weill Cornell's highly regarded Department of Neurology and Neuroscience. I ultimately hope to participate in the M.D. with Honors in Research program.

New York City is also very attractive. The diverse range of patients undoubtedly offers great clinical education. Furthermore, I have lived in rural and suburban areas all my life, so living in an urban area would be a completely new experience. The plethora of exciting opportunities, both academic and otherwise, at Weill Cornell and in New York would surely fuel my professional and personal development.

At the University of Michigan Medical School, we are committed to building a superb educational community with students of diverse talents, experiences, opinions, and backgrounds. What would you as an individual bring to our medical school community?

My childhood healer, Master Huang, practiced traditional Chinese medicine. He alleviated nearly every sports injury that I developed as a young athlete by utilizing a combination of acupuncture, ancient Chinese fire-heated cupping, and chi therapy. Growing up in an immigrant family where traditional Chinese medicine was a major part of life, I have gained first-hand experiences with alternative medicine and have developed a strong cultural sensitivity as a result of this exposure. I will bring to the University of Michigan Medical School, a unique perspective of the inner-workings of traditional Chinese medicine and an understanding that many patients may have grown up in diverse cultures with various medical frameworks.

While most of my early healthcare experiences involved Integrative Medicine, I have also completely immersed myself into studying the intricacies of Western medicine and basic science. As part of my two-year cancer research, I have identified up-regulated pathways in tumor blood vessels and conducted novel experiments that elucidated how tumors metastasize and grow to invade other tissues. Furthermore, I have also been designing experiments that aim to determine whether low oxygen levels in pancreatic endocrine tumors may contribute to their aggressive nature. I will bring to the University of Michigan a strong background in basic science research and an enthusiastic drive to work in a team and perform cutting-edge research.

Why the OUWB School of Medicine? And why you?

I was absolutely thrilled to learn about the OUWB Capstone Project. This unique four-year curriculum presents a wonderful opportunity for me to continue pursuing my passions in cancer research and community outreach. My goal is to drive innovation in cutting-edge research and bring cost-effective cancer therapies to underserved populations. In my current cancer research, I have identified up-regulated pathways in tumor blood vessels and conducted novel experiments that elucidated how tumors metastasize and grow to invade other tissues. Collaborating with scientists and doctors in both academia and industry has prepared me to continue such professional partnerships as a future scientist and student at OUWB. Furthermore, my deep scientific curiosity and solid understanding of experimental design will enable me to spearhead innovative projects at the Beaumont Research Institute.

Beyond my strong interests in cancer research, my volunteer experiences at multiple free clinics have prepared me to serve the diverse communities of Michigan. Closely listening to and connecting with patients at these free clinics has enabled me to gain a broad perspective of the public health issues in America today. I will merge this perspective with my passion for service to drive initiatives at OUWB that meet society's most dire needs.

OUWB's integrated curriculum is ideal because it complements my hands-on learning style and incorporates medicine in a social context. I am particularly attracted to the organ system approach, which combines basic science learning with clinical practice throughout all four years. I value that this integration fosters a team environment where I can work closely with classmates and faculty to actively problem-solve in the classroom and the clinic.

Name: Debbie Chen

At Rosalind Franklin University, we celebrate and support a Life in Discovery. Briefly describe what a Life in Discovery means to you.

To me, a Life in Discovery is a way of life. It is nurtured through an unrelenting curiosity and persistent desire to explore the unknown. A Life in Discovery embodies the mentality of leaders within medicine whose goals are to care for and improve mankind. Driving this progress within the medical field requires multiple interdisciplinary teams to work together and establish innovative ways to advance medicine and optimize healthcare. I view a Life in Discovery as a lifestyle that I am currently embodying and would like to continue pursuing in my future medical career at Rosalind Franklin University of Medicine and Science.

Leaders in the research realm live a Life in Discovery by approaching the world with an unparalleled inquisitiveness. Following through with their questions, these scientists have the optimism and creativity to innovate experiments that are designed to produce answers. Discovery in the clinical realm involves learning about another human being's cultural background, belief systems, and interests to establish strong relationships that foster teamwork. I envision this teamwork eventually resulting in future novel discoveries. Finally, inspiring younger generations to navigate the uncharted waters of a Life in Discovery is an integral part of continuing this tradition that Rosalind Franklin began half a century ago.

The risk of embodying a Life in Discovery is high, as it encourages venturing into a place where no one else has gone before. This is a risk that I will continue to take since I know that each failure along the way is an integral part of the process of discovery. I see the Rosalind Franklin University Medical School as an important part of my journey to fulfill a Life in Discovery as I pursue my goals in academic medicine. Inspired by Rosalind Franklin, I will tirelessly pioneer cutting-edge innovations in research, compassionately care for diverse human conditions in the clinic, and passionately mentor younger generations in academia to live Lives in Discovery.

Name: Rachel Rizal

Please write a brief statement giving your reasons for applying to Weill Cornell Medical College.

The integrative curriculum and emphasis on global health set Weill Cornell Medical College apart from other medical schools. Cornell's curriculum complements my multidisciplinary approach, because it puts medicine in a broader social context and incorporates policy topics. At Princeton's Woodrow Wilson School, I pursued classes and activities to examine the intersection of medicine with public health, public policy, and business. At Cornell, I will deepen my understanding of healthcare complexities, enabling me to improve medical care, especially in underserved communities. I will be involved in the forefront of research and projects with the departments of Infectious Diseases, Prevention & Health Behavior, and Health Policy.

Cornell will deepen my expertise in global health. During my Fulbright Fellowship in the Philippines, I gained tremendous insight about healthcare in developing countries. I diagnosed cervical cancer in low-resource settings and assisted in bringing the HPV vaccine into a national healthcare program. Building on my experiences, I will get involved with cervical cancer screening and prevention initiatives in the Office of Global Health Education. The opportunity to work closely with my Professors excites me. I am eager to learn from my colleagues and to share my insights about global health with others.

DIVERSITY ESSAYS

Remember that when a school asks about your diverse background experiences, this does not necessarily mean your ethnic / family background. We've read many essays that talk about somebody's experiences abroad – for example, building a public health education program in Ecuador. Others have talked about growing up in the heart of Bronx and how those experiences have shaped their outlooks on healthcare and the world. Think broadly about your life experiences and we hope that these essays can give you some ideas about the array of topics you can write about!

Name: Mike Baxter

How will you contribute to the diversity of your medical school class and the University of Virginia School of Medicine?

I believe that I will be able to contribute to the diversity of UVA through the variety and depth of my experience, if not through familial background. Since before high school, I have had a special interest in Latin America and the Spanish language. In the past few years my interest in Latin American culture and politics has grown with the opportunities I have had to travel and study abroad.

Much of my exposure to the Spanish language and Latin American culture has come from Hispanic immigrants living and working in my community. I was always impressed by the great number of Latino immigrants working from before the sun came up until long after dark. Their lives were made even more difficult if they spoke little or no English. While I did not speak a word of Spanish growing up, fluency became a goal of mine in

132

high school as I realized it was the only way to really learn about their unique perspectives and backgrounds. Since then, I have made myself fluent and now I can do everything from translating for Spanish speaking patients to ordering dinner in a Peruvian restaurant. This learning has paid real dividends in terms the hundreds of people who I have met both in the U.S. and abroad. Additionally, having a semester to live in Colombia as the Colombians live altered my own attitudes. I learned what it was like to be the minority in a foreign and frequently confusing land.

I know I could contribute to UVA's diversity both through what I have already experienced and through my desire to broaden my knowledge of other countries and peoples. I hope to continue to deepen my understanding of Latin America and add to the diversity of the student body of UVA.

Name: Mike Baxter

If applicable, describe a situation where you were not in the majority.

Over the last year I spent over six months in various parts of Latin America. My travels included my exchange semester in Colombia, a medical rotation in Peru, and personal travel in Argentina. Naturally, I found it difficult to assimilate at first. Having blond hair and only mediocre language skills, I had to work hard to fit in. In Colombia this was of particular concern due to the kidnappings and other security risks. In other places I was routinely charged higher prices as an obvious non-local customer. As my Spanish improved and I learned more of the local customs I learned to fit in much better and I really enjoyed the experience. After my return, I've worked hard to help visitors to our country understanding much better the barriers that sometimes exist.

Briefly describe a situation where you had to overcome adversity; include lessons learned and how you think it will affect your career as a future physician.

During the fall of 2007 I was selected to participate in an exchange program with the Colombian Naval Academy in Cartagena, Colombia. After I arrived in Colombia I quickly found that their officer development program was very dysfunctional and there were many injustices. After enduring this situation for weeks I began to document and discuss these issues in a constructive way with members of the administration and student body. At first they were not receptive and sometimes even hostile. However, some changes were eventually made and we saw some improvements by the end of our semester there. Watching morale improve confirmed that taking the initiative and confronting difficult issues was the correct course. I know that I will experience similar situations as a physician and I feel that my experience in Colombia will help me to address similar situations in the future.

Name: Rachel Rizal

Briefly describe a situation where you had to overcome adversity; include lessons learned and how you think it will affect your career as a future physician.

I founded Health Matters to provide health resources to low-income families in Princeton, NJ. Educating Spanish-speaking children and their parents was very challenging. At first, we failed to attract parents, and it was difficult to plan engaging activities for kids at various ages. To solve this, we personally spoke to each parent, provided free dinners solicited from restaurants, and brought bilingual doctors. We had to be more creative with our workshops. Kids measured heart rates when playing "Simon Says." We added family cooking lessons. As a result, families told us about their lifestyle changes, such as improving their diets and joining sports. Health Matters taught me that there are multiple approaches to changing a person's health, and they can involve experimentation and creativity. As a physician, I will be persistent when leading programs even during difficult circumstances.

Name: Rachel Rizal

If applicable, describe a situation you were not the majority.

I was invited to a meeting with influential doctors and policymakers in the Philippines. They were finalizing the Secretary of Health's national address on the current state and future direction of healthcare. I was the only female, non-resident, and the most inexperienced person in the room. But, the group welcomed my opinions. I gave suggestions on improving the visual presentation and diction of the speech.

During his speech, I wondered, "Why are you advocating universal healthcare coverage even though it is impossible for the government to finance this?" I hesitated to ask this question, fearing that it undermined the speech's message. Finally, I could not contain my curiosity. Dr. D explained, "If we push for the realistic 10% coverage, the government will only cover 1%. But, if we push for 100%, the government will agree to 10%." His answer was inspirational.

Because I took the initiative to speak out, everyone benefited that day. I learned that in order to influence great changes globally, I should never be afraid to have a bold vision and share it with others.

The Committee on Admissions strongly encourages you to share unique, personally important, and/or challenging factors in your background, such as the quality of your early educational environment, socioeconomic status, culture, race, ethnicity, sexual orientation, or life or work experiences. Please discuss how such factors have influenced your goals and preparation for a career in medicine.

I intensely protested when my dad told my family we were moving to America. We had already moved houses in England three times so I was constantly leaving friends every few years. This upset was compounded by the challenge of having to adjust to an entirely new culture and environment in America. Having moved from Switzerland to England to America as part of a Chinese immigrant family, I have assumed many different cultural identities along the way. Only after moving to America did I learn to manage and fully identify with each of these unique identities.

When it came time to apply to college, I was unsure about checking the box for 'Asian-American'. As it happened, the Stanford application did not have a box for 'Asian' or 'Chinese', which is what I more readily identified with in terms of ethnicity. However, after naturalizing as an American citizen, becoming more involved in the Asian American community on campus, and learning more about race and medicine, I realized that the use of 'Asian-American' and terms like it is incredibly arbitrary. Moreover, I learned about the dangers in medicine of either conflating race with ancestry or perceiving race as culture. Through this exercise though, I came to understand and embrace my own cultural and ethnic heritage and be more cognizant of the multitude of experiences that have shaped each one of us.

So despite my initial protest of moving to America, the experience of becoming a Swiss-born-Asian-American-Chinese-Brit has prepared me to interact with the increasingly diverse patients and communities of an increasingly globalized world. It has also influenced me to be more sensitive to each of our cultural backgrounds. Especially in medicine, having this cultural awareness and empathy is something I hope to bring with me to my practice in the future. America is my home now and I consider myself American, but I will always remember my many identities in order to be the best doctor that I can be.

Name: Rishi Mediratta

The Committee on Admissions strongly encourages you to share unique, personally important, and/or challenging factors in your background, such as the quality of your early educational environment, socioeconomic status, culture, race, ethnicity, sexual orientation, or life or work experiences. Please discuss how such factors have influenced your goals and preparation for a career in medicine.

Inspired by my meeting with Dr. Hodes at the airport, I spent the winter break of my sophomore year living with the Hodes family. I immediately bonded with the 15 sick orphans in the house. They taught me Amharic, I helped them with their homework, we ate Injera and Shuro together, played soccer, and danced to traditional music. Getting to know the orphans made me want to learn more about the unique culture and the relationship between culture and health.

I returned to Ethiopia to study the risk factors and management of diarrhea in a community of Jewish Ethiopians. I discovered the majority of mothers withheld fluids from their children during diarrheal episodes. To understand this dangerous practice, I convened a focus group to grasp how local health beliefs affect children's health. Ethiopians believe that health results from equilibrium between the body and the external world, and sickness results from an imbalance between these forces. Mothers were withholding fluids from their children because they were trying to prevent further fluid loss, thereby thinking they were restoring equilibrium. These discussions resulted in my designing a pictograph that incorporated the concept of equilibrium with increasing fluid intake during diarrheal episodes.

Living in Ethiopia for six months over the last three years, I not only learned the language and health beliefs, but also applied my sensitivity of the culture towards solving a medical problem. I gained insight into culturally appropriate strategies to improve the Ethiopian health care system-knowledge that I will translate into practice as I dedicate my life to improving the health of Ethiopian children. My understanding about the ways in which culture influences health will effectively prepare me as a physician to communicate with patients from diverse backgrounds. At Stanford, I hope to continue finding ways to close the gap between knowledge and practice by pursuing approaches that merge culture with medicine.

*At the University of Michigan Medical School,
we are committed to building a superb
educational community with students of
diverse talents, experiences, opinions, and
backgrounds. What would you as an
individual bring to our medical school
community?*

My parents started our lives in the United States with only \$100. In the beginning, our furniture consisted of used couches found on the side of road and old bed sheets draped over cardboard boxes. We often had to take baths at our friends' houses because our own water had turned brown. Even before my parents separated, my father was rarely around, so my mother essentially raised me alone. In addition to caring for me, she also waited tables during the day and studied English at night. It was exhausting, but my mother never complained; instead, she taught me the value of hard work and perseverance as she painstakingly bettered our lives. At the same time, she pushed me to pursue my goals and instilled within me a desire to continuously improve myself even in the face challenges. While our current situation is by no means perfect, it is hard to believe how far we have come. As a result of my childhood experiences and witnessing my mother's struggles, I have developed a greater sensitivity toward others. Every person has their own unique story, and I enjoy taking the time to understand the foundations of their perspectives. I have also learned to appreciate not only what others have done in the past, but also what they are striving to do in the future. I hope to bring these characteristics to medical school and help my peers achieve their goals even as I am working toward my own.

The Admissions Committee is interested in gaining further insight into you as a person. Please describe the experience which you found most personally challenging to this point in your life and discuss how it helped shape you as a person. You may discuss a moral or ethical dilemma, situation of personal adversity or other life-event you believe to have been an important hurdle for you.

In many ways, I embody characteristics of the stereotypical Asian. Love science and math? Check. Play piano or violin? Double check (I play both). Relish bargain sales? Definitely check.

However, I am more multidimensional than any single stereotype. For instance, I enrolled in the "Arts in Contemporary Society" FOCUS (first-year seminar) program and happily immersed myself in creative writing and music courses, instead of enrolling in the science-themed programs. And though active in Duke's Asian Students' Association, I have an incredibly diverse group of friends and avoid self-segregation. My identity is not defined by being Asian.

This was not always true. Growing up in Kokomo, Indiana from age 5 to 13, I was the only Chinese girl in my school. Though my classmates occasionally teased me about my small eyes or the "weird stuff" I had for lunch, in general they were very friendly. Still, I knew I stuck out despite my perfect English and Midwestern upbringing. I also struggled with the clash of two different sets of cultural values: one immigrant Chinese, and the other white Middle America.

My racial otherness diminished upon moving to California and has not been an issue in college either. However, there is one area where my race has re-emerged: athletics. When I tried out for the track team in 9th grade, a few of my classmates balked. "Asians aren't good athletes," they claimed.

Determined to disprove them, I became one of the top vaulters in California and was officially recruited to several collegiate programs. As an Asian-American NCAA Division I student-athlete, I am still a minority and still encounter occasional racist jokes. But instead of developing fruitless anger, I channel my energy toward simply doing my personal best. Ultimately, I do not want my race to define me, in athletics or in life.

But my biggest challenge has been the task of simply being a student-athlete, regardless of race. In high school, I started at the very bottom of our training group. The pole vault's technicality and complexity eluded me, and I almost quit before my second season. But I still enjoyed learning about the sport, and with encouraging family and coaches behind me, I stayed on and slowly improved after countless hours of extra practice, developing callused hands and an iron will.

In college, technique is no longer my greatest foe. Instead, it is balancing academics and athletics when both areas demand greater intensity than before. My first collegiate track season was particularly difficult. I trained every weekday and traveled to meets every weekend. The physical demands were obvious, but I underestimated the mental demands of missing classes and juggling everything. Constantly stressed, I did not sleep well. My athletic performance suffered. Again, I considered quitting.

But first, I sought Duke's time management counseling services and made sleep a top priority. Eventually, I regained balance and stayed on the team. Over the past few years, I have vaulted well enough to compete at several elite meets and secure a spot on Duke's all-time Top 5 list while maintaining my academics as well.

Pole vaulting has taught me perseverance, prioritization, and problem-solving. These skills have also helped with challenging coursework, research, and even my personal life.

Though I only have one year of vaulting left, I am sure the lessons learned as a student-athlete will last and carry me through as I pursue a medical career.

Name: Sally Baxter

Briefly describe a situation where you had to overcome adversity; include lessons learned and how you think it will affect your career as a future physician.

My first collegiate track season was challenging. I trained every weekday and then traveled to meets virtually every weekend. The physical demands were obvious, but I underestimated the mental demands of missing classes and juggling everything. Constantly stressed, I did not sleep well. My athletic performance suffered. I considered quitting, which was common for first-year athletes.

But first, I sought time management counseling from Duke's Academic Skills Instructional Program and made sleep a top priority. Eventually, I regained balance and decided to stay on the team, later improving my vaulting skills while still maintaining my academics. From that experience, I learned the values of perseverance, resilience, and prioritization, and how to cope with stress. These lessons have carried me through college and will surely help me face future adversity as I pursue a medical career.

If Applicable, describe a situation where you were not in the majority.

Growing up in Kokomo, IN from age 5 to 13, I was the only Chinese girl in my school district. I was sometimes teased about my small eyes or the "weird stuff" I brought for lunch. Despite my perfect English and Midwestern upbringing, I was oftentimes pigeonholed as "the Chinese girl". I also grappled with the clash of two cultures, something my white friends did not understand.

My racial otherness diminished upon moving to California and has not been an issue in college either. However, there is one area where my race has re-emerged: athletics. When I tried out for the track team in 9th grade, a few of my classmates balked. "Asians aren't good athletes," they claimed.

I was determined to disprove them. I became one of the top vaulters in the state and was officially recruited to Duke. Now, as an Asian-American NCAA Division I student-athlete, I am still a minority and still encounter occasional racist jokes. But instead of developing fruitless anger, I channel my energy toward simply doing my personal best. Ultimately, I do not want my race to define me, in athletics or in life.

OTHER ACTIVITIES

Do you have any other activities or achievements that you want the Admissions Office to know about? Some schools allow you to talk about other activities that are meaningful to you.

Our advice: *Try to talk about activities that you haven't written about in your AMCAS Personal Statement.*

Name: Mike Baxter

Briefly describe your most rewarding experience or some achievement of which you are particularly proud.

I have found my volunteer work in the medical field to be extraordinarily rewarding. Preparing meals, repairing houses, and tutoring students in the past through my school, church, and Boy Scouts helped disadvantaged people to some degree, but I was often left not knowing how much our work really helped. My work at Baltimore Shock Trauma, in a free clinic in Annapolis, and as part of a Navy medical team in South America allowed me to see a direct, visible, and immediate benefit conferred on patients with urgent, sometimes desperate needs. Participating even in a minor way in the care of a multiple gunshot wound victim certain to die without immediate and extraordinarily complex care has been both inspiring and rewarding. Helping the poorest of Columbia's children receive basic medical care was rewarding beyond words and something which has very strongly reinforced my desire to become a physician.

Dance Marathon

I first became involved in Dance Marathon as a morale captain my freshman and sophomore years. As a morale captain, I was responsible for organizing a team of dancers, creating the Morale Dance, and providing support for the executive board. I spent an average of 3 hours a week attending morale captain meetings and planning team fundraising activities. I arranged canning shifts at a local Wal-Mart, coordinated a "Breakfast for Dinner" meal fundraiser, and worked with other morale captains to host the first Dance Marathon Date Auction. During my junior and senior years, I served on the executive board as the External Public Relations Chair and Entertainment Chair, respectively. As a member of the executive board, my commitment during the year was approximately 6 hours a week, but was over 30 hours the week of the event.

Chi Omega

I joined Chi Omega in 2006. During the new member period, my commitment was approximately 5 hours a week. That same semester and in the next spring, I was a cast member in my chapter's production for Thurtene, the annual student-run charity carnival. In the weeks leading up to the event, I spent an additional 6 to 8 hours a week rehearsing and two full days performing at the carnival. I also chaired the Senior Farewell committee in the spring of 2007. While I was abroad in November 2007, I was slated as the Recruitment Chair for the 2008 calendar year. Throughout that year, I worked closely with seven other executive board members, my Recruitment Advisor, and recruitment chairs from the other chapters. I also supervised an Assistant Recruitment Chair as well as a committee of twenty members holding various positions. During the spring of 2008, my commitment was an average of 10 hours a week but ranged from 12 to over 24 hours a week in the fall semester.

Gateway Teaching Assistant

I served as an Anatomy and Physiology teaching assistant at Gateway Institute of Technology High School as part of a new service learning program through the Biology Department. My overarching responsibility was to help develop the course as well as the role of the teaching assistant. I spent 6 hours a week in the classroom coordinating projects with the teacher, advising students, and teaching joint lessons with the other teaching assistant. An additional 4 to 5 hours a week was required outside of class for prep work. I also designed and implemented a weekly journaling routine to help monitor student progress and receive feedback on our lessons throughout the semester.

Name: Taylor Hobson

What is the ONE most important honor you have received? Why do you view this as important?

This past academic year, I was selected to the Pac-10 Conference All-Academic Team for both the indoor and outdoor track seasons. As a member of the UCLA Men's Track & Field team and a Physiological Sciences major, I compete with some of the top athletes and students in the country. Time spent traveling and competing in meets throughout the country has caused me to miss valuable in-class lecture time and take examinations on the road while also preparing to compete in the top track & field events in the country. I have worked hard to balance these activities so this recognition was rewarding because of all of the hard work and discipline required to achieve it.

*What has been the most scholarly project
(thesis, research, or field of study in basic or
clinical science or in the humanities)?
Describe one and give number of hours, dates
and advisor.*

Since the end of June, I have been working in the MacDonald Research Lab on the campus of UCLA with Dr. Sharon Hame. Our most recent research project is on temporal trends in the number of arthroscopic hip procedures done from 2004-2009. This project required 25 hours/week to gather, sort, and analyze all of the statistics. By cross-referencing CPT and ICD-9 codes related to the hip, we were able to break the numbers down by region, gender, and age using the PearlDiver Patient Records Database. We have written the full article and have submitted it for publication. We will continue using the PearlDiver Database in future studies and have recently received software for dynamic MRI's which will be a new source for future research projects and provide me early exposure to studying MRI's.

Name: Sally Baxter

Research

For my project in Nina Sherwood's lab, I examined the effects of cold temperature on fly models of autosomal dominant hereditary spastic paraplegia (AD-HSP), which decreases motor function in affected humans. Mutations in the spastin gene account for 50-60% of AD-HSP cases. Spastin encodes a microtubule (MT)-severing protein, but little is known about the mechanisms by which its mutations cause AD-HSP.

Spastin null flies, which have the spastin gene deleted, exhibit decreased eclosion rate (emergence of the adult fly from the pupal case), climb rate, and lifespan compared to wild-type flies. These deficits seemed to lessen when the null flies were raised at reduced temperatures. My task was to further investigate this striking observation. Since MTs disassemble in the cold, I hypothesized that cold-induced MT disassembly might substitute for spastin's MT-severing function to yield an improved phenotype.

I subjected 2 spastin null fly lines and 1 transgenic fly line expressing mutant human spastin to cold treatment at different developmental stages. I then measured the flies' eclosion rate, their motor function using a climb rate assay, and their survival by recording lifespan. Larval stage cold treatment exerted no significant beneficial effect. However, pupal stage cold treatment significantly improved eclosion rate, climb rate, and lifespan for all 3 fly lines compared to untreated controls! Adult stage cold treatment also significantly improved climb rate in 1 null line and in the transgenic line.

These improvements signal promise for the development of cold-based therapies for AD-HSP patients. There are also implications for basic understanding of spastin function in the fly, which is currently limited. For instance, though the behavioral phenotype of spastin null flies is severe and well-characterized, the cellular phenotype is completely unknown. To explore what cellular changes may underlie the more readily observed behavioral changes, I have been dissecting null fly brains, staining them with antibodies labeling certain neuronal subsets, and comparing these brains to those of wild-type flies. By subsequently examining the cold's effects in this cellular context, we might determine a mechanism of cold action, thus deepening our understanding of MT regulation and its relationship to AD-HSP.

Through this experience, summer research projects, working in academic medical environments, and local- and national-level presentations, I have witnessed how critical research is to medicine and have experienced the entire scientific process from posing questions to communicating results. Presenting one's work leads to an exchange of ideas that generates more questions, leading to more experiments and results, and so on. Instead of being linear, it is a spiral: a cyclical process that becomes more focused over time. The journey is rarely straightforward, and I have experienced firsthand the obstacles that arise in research. However, the thrill of discovery and ultimate potential to promote health still trump any frustrations in the interim.

My mentors have also inspired me. They are great role models who reassure me it is possible to balance a research career with family life. I also have my own experience balancing D1 athletics with courses, research, and other activities. With my undergraduate preparation, clinical and research experience, and supportive mentors, I am prepared and excited about pursuing a career as a physician investigator.

Pole Vaulting

Pole vaulting for Duke's track and field team has been a demanding yet amazing experience. My body is pushed to its limits during our fall conditioning workouts of weightlifting, sprinting/running, and pole vaulting. Training consumes 3-4 hours per day, 5 days a week. In the spring, workouts are just as long, but they are milder in intensity so as to not tire us out for weekly meets. I have competed every indoor and outdoor season since starting college. Though training and competing can be exhausting, I am so grateful to be an NCAA Division I athlete who has access to outstanding opportunities both on the field and in the classroom. Being an athlete has also taught me lessons in time management, teamwork, and perseverance. Plus, nothing beats the feeling of flying up high into the air.

FUTURE

Some schools want your insights into your future career (either short-term or long term) or about the future of medicine.

Name: Mike Baxter

What do you think will be your greatest personal challenge as a physician, and how will you address this?

I have spent almost half of the past year in various parts of Latin America; from an exchange semester in Colombia to a medical rotation in Peru to personal travel in Argentina. Everywhere I go in South America, I rapidly find myself the lone "yanqui" or "gringo" in a crowd of Latino Americans. At first it was difficult simply because of my mediocre Spanish and ignorance of daily life in South American countries. Having blondish hair and blue eyes usually prevents me from blending in physically, but I began to assimilate in every other possible way. And considering the kidnappings of foreigners that have taken place in Colombia, it was very important to me to avoid standing out. Of a less grave nature was the way I was treated in society. When I went to buy something in the market or take a taxi I was often charged an inflated price as a result of my appearance. But once I became more fluent in both their language and culture I was able to deal with them less as a foreigner and on a more equal footing.

Are there any areas of medicine that are of particular interest to you? If so, please comment.

I find the field of infectious diseases to be very interesting. I In working at Baltimore Shock Trauma, I have seen incredibly skilled physicians deal with multiple drug resistant Tuberculosis and S. aureus. In Colombia and Peru I met local doctors who were treating diseases rarely seen in the U.S. such as Chaga's Disease, dengue fever, and malaria. Working with the Navy's Malaria Vaccine Program last summer and the Naval Medical Research Center in Iquitos in the Amazon Basin this summer has reinforced my interest in this field. Additionally, I would like to obtain education in public health to enable me to combat disease on a population wide scale.

Name: Taylor Hobson

Where do you see yourself in 10 years? What experiences have led you to this goal?

In 10 years, I will be a physician practicing in various underserved communities, providing members of these communities with the proper healthcare that they need to live healthy lifestyles. Outside of my work as a physician, I will continue to actively participate in community service opportunities, including mentoring programs where I can advocate the importance of education. I hope to have developed a scholarship fund that will provide financial support to youth from underserved communities who are interested in pursuing a medical degree. I will have a wife and possibly children. My experiences as a student-athlete, giving back to underserved communities, and growing up in a well-balanced and supportive home are just a few of the experiences that have led to and shaped my goals.

Name: Rishi Mediratta

Which area of medicine do you see yourself pursuing? Why?

I am well suited for a career in public health because of the knowledge and skills I obtained at the Bloomberg School of Public Health, my extensive clinical experiences in Ethiopia, and my commitment to helping Ethiopian children. As a public health major, I analyzed health situations in developing countries and made evidence-based recommendations; learned how to conduct behavior change interventions; and gained insight into nutritional deficiencies and infectious diseases plaguing children. I applied these skills while researching diarrheal disease in Ethiopia and designing a health education intervention. This work taught me that I could save the lives of children by training as a physician and public health scientist. As a physician, I will dedicate time to the Ethiopian Orphan Health Foundation and continue improving the health of Ethiopian children. A career in public health will allow me to fulfill my dream to design, implement, and manage child survival programs in Ethiopia.

Name: Debbie Chen

Why have you chosen to apply to Georgetown University School of Medicine, and how do you think your education at Georgetown will prepare you to become a physician for the future?

The service-oriented medical education and cura personalis philosophy at Georgetown perfectly complement my desire to become a physician who cares about all aspects of a patient's life. Reflecting on my experiences in the sport of synchronized swimming, I was a teammate and leader who was constantly aware of the physical and mental states of the team. Serving as a team captain at Stanford, I led not only by motivating teammates in the pool, but also by attending to the unique circumstances in each of my teammate's lives. I was aware of each teammate's background, and tailored my supportive actions and words towards their personal needs. I wish to apply the "whole person" perspective that I have gained in athletics to my future career in medicine. I cannot imagine a more fitting medical school than Georgetown to help me achieve this goal.

Due to my passion for athletics, I am a strong believer that the mind and body are intricately connected determinants of health. I was absolutely thrilled to learn about the Mind Body Medicine program in Georgetown's curriculum. With chronic disease cases on the rise, preventative medicine will be integral to the future of American healthcare. By offering students this Mind Body course, Georgetown is leading an integral initiative to incorporate patient self-awareness and education in healthcare.

Through serving the uninsured and homeless populations at various free clinics, I have realized that my passion for medicine does not stop at providing quality bedside

153

care. I wish to be an active patient advocate in our healthcare system. For this reason, I am very interested in pursuing the Health Justice Scholar Track at Georgetown. Through engaging in this elective and conducting an advocacy research project, I know that I will gain unique perspectives of my role as a future healthcare provider. This perspective will enable me to become a physician who promotes social justice in healthcare at the heart of our nation, Washington DC.

Representing Georgetown as a community health advocate is just as important to me as serving medically disadvantaged populations in the clinic. The Hoya Clinic, in particular, will enable me to continue serving members of the homeless and uninsured communities. Through my close interactions with individuals from underserved populations, I have experienced first-hand, how health disparities drastically affect health outcomes. I hope to dedicate myself to helping Washington DC's underserved communities by combining my passion for service with my experience in cancer research to spearhead cancer-screening initiatives at the Hoya Clinic.

As I work to increase basic healthcare access for underserved populations, I also have a strong desire to pursue research opportunities through the Lombardi Comprehensive Cancer Center. I am incredibly impressed with the Georgetown Database of Cancer, which allows physicians and scientists to tailor cancer treatments to individual patients. By utilizing technology and molecular science to predict responses to cancer treatment, I believe that Georgetown is at the forefront of alleviating the increasing burden that cancer is placing on our society. I look forward to building upon my current cancer research experiences by pursuing involvement in these innovative research projects at the Lombardi Comprehensive Cancer Center.

Georgetown truly contains all the components of my ideal medical school. I desire to be the compassionate physician who can alleviate clinical diseases while also attending to the overall experience of human pain. Alongside, I wish to be a physician-scientist who is knowledgeable of the molecular intricacies of drug therapies and serves humanity by advancing medicine through research. I firmly believe that Georgetown's curriculum, service opportunities, and world-class research institutions will provide me with the tools to achieve these goals. I wish to attend Georgetown to be trained under the philosophy of cura personalis to become the best doctor I can be.

Name: Rachel Rizal

Are there any areas of medicine which you are particularly proud?

Dr. M's "Infection" class crystallized in my mind that lowering the burden of illness from infectious diseases takes the efforts of doctors, pharmaceutical companies, governments, and NGOs. I became excited about these synergies, which inspired my senior thesis research and Fulbright projects on preventing infectious diseases.

My senior thesis examined new vaccine introduction in middle-income countries. I discovered that the Hepatitis B vaccine was introduced in the Philippines earlier than in most developed nations because a small, dedicated team of hepatologists pushed the government to provide vaccines for babies. I realized that a few doctors could make a huge impact; during my Fulbright, I was motivated to assist in bringing the new HPV vaccine into a Philippines health program.

I feel that there is much potential for innovative medicines to be dispersed to people with limited healthcare access. I believe my background in policy and business will allow me to integrate ideas from these fields with medicine to successfully combat infectious diseases in the future.

In the celebrity culture of my native Southern California, we often speak of the 'triple threat': a star who can sing, dance, and act. My career goal is to be a different kind of triple threat - a physician who excels at patient care, research, and education. There is no greater satisfaction than to help improve some-one's health. Having had transformative clinical experiences at the Duke Brain Tumor Center and at a Chinese academic hospital, I would like to directly provide medical care to patients in the future. I am also passionate about research. Whether it is investigating the genetics of spastic paraplegia, stem cell development, the effects of stress on myelination, or the psychosocial effects of vision loss, I delight in the process of asking questions and expanding knowledge. I know firsthand that results are often hard-earned. However, the ultimate reward of learning something previously unknown, thereby moving medicine forward, trumps any frustrations in the interim. Finally, having served as an English language teacher to Latino immigrants and as a peer advisor to my classmates, I have tasted the immense gratification of teaching and advising and hope to be involved in medical education during my career. Besides my personal experience in these areas, I have also worked with some physician 'stars' who are true triple threats and have made extraordinary contributions to the world. Their examples have further inspired me to pursue an academic medical career.

Made in the USA
San Bernardino, CA
01 December 2018